GARDENING

A Beginner's Guide

Need — 2 — Know

Angela Youngman

D1465239

First published in Great Britain in 2011 by
Need2Know
Remus House
Coltsfoot Drive
Peterborough
PE2 9JX
Telephone 01733 898103
Fax 01733 313524
www.need2knowbooks.co.uk

Need2Know is an imprint of Bonacia Ltd.
www.forwardpoetry.co.uk
SB ISBN 978-1-86144-100-3
Cover photograph: Dreamstime

Contents

Introduction

Every year large numbers of people find themselves with a garden that they do not know how to care for or use effectively, it may be as a result of buying a house for the first time, or taking on an allotment in order to grow food. In addition, there are increasing numbers of people wanting to grow their own vegetables within their existing garden.

If you're one of these people finding yourself a bit baffled by garden experts in the media, who often complicate the process of gardening with Latin names and exhaustive details, you may be a bit scared of gardening or trying new things in case you get it wrong. It is important to remember in many areas of gardening, there is no absolute right or wrong, all that matters is what works for you. Every garden expert has had their share of disasters and they never stop having them either.

Yet most people, when faced with a garden or allotment for the first time, find it a nerve-racking experience. Just what can you do with the space? How do you care for the plants? What can you grow? This book aims to provide the simple, basic information necessary to start gardening such as, what equipment you need and how to choose it, recommendations on easy to grow plants and vegetables, and basic techniques and what to do if things go wrong.

Visiting a garden centre or nursery can make you think that you have to spend lots of money; however all you really need to start are a few tools and plants. Basic, easily understood information is essential. It can be extremely difficult and off putting when you look at the vast ranges of equipment in a garden centre and wonder which brand to get and which tools you need for your garden project. This book covers the many ways you can save money in your garden by bargain hunting and recycling materials and plants – it helps the environment too.

Gardening has lots of advantages:

- Digging and caring for a garden regularly can use up as much energy as going to a gym, it's an easy and relaxing way to contribute to a healthy lifestyle.

- You can grow your own food; you know exactly how fresh it is and where it has come from – zero food miles helps the environment and there is nothing as tasty and satisfying as tucking in to your own fresh veg.

- A nice garden can increase the value of your house and create a much more pleasant environment in which to live

- Being out and about in nature is wonderful – sometimes it brings you amazing crops and surprises, sometimes, even when you have done everything correctly, nature lets you down, but that variety and uncertainty is part of the fun.

- However, the most important thing is that gardening is enjoyable and satisfying.

So, regardless of what size garden you have this simple self-help guide is for anyone who wants to give it a go but doesn't quite know where to start – I hope you find it a helpful and informative starting point.

Happy gardening!

Disclaimer

Caution should be exercised when using specialist equipment or substances in your garden, ensure you carefully follow the instructions given on the packaging, especially if they are different to the processes described in this book.

Chapter One

Where to Start

Taking over a new garden when you don't have a lot of gardening expertise or experience can seem a daunting task. Just what do you do with the bare space around your home? If you already have a garden, how do you care for it and adjust the garden to your needs?

Thankfully, it is not difficult – all you need is some time, patience and the right tools, and working through this book will give you the knowledge necessary to look after your garden.

Choosing your equipment

Having the right tools to do the job makes a big difference. But it can be overwhelming to go into a garden centre and see racks of spades, forks, hoes and other seemingly miscellaneous garden items. How do you choose and what do you really need?

Gardening equipment

For a first time gardener, the most essential tools are:

- A digging fork and spade.
- A hoe.
- A soil rake.
- A wheelbarrow.

'All you need is some time, patience and the right tools, and working through this book will give you the knowledge necessary to look after your garden.'

- A hand fork and trowel.
- Secateurs.
- Loppers.
- Shears.
- A dibber (type of hand tool).
- A sharpening tool.
- String.
- Labels.
- Permanent marker pen.
- Pots and seed trays.

'When you choose tools, take care to make sure they are the right weight for you. There can be a vast difference between the weight of various brands of spade or loppers and using a tool that is too heavy for a long period can be extremely tiring.'

When you choose tools, take care to make sure they are the right weight for you. There can be a vast difference between the weight of various brands of spade or loppers and using a tool that is too heavy for a long period can be extremely tiring.

Visit a garden centre and take the tools off the racks and try using them.

- Secateurs – make sure the safety catch can be reached easily, ideally with one hand.

- Loppers may be needed for cutting branches above head height, which means you will have to hold them high, putting pressure on your arms – so try them at different angles to see which loppers feel most comfortable to you. As you test them for weight, also consider the grip on the handles. Some people find sponge covered handles more comfortable, other people are happy with metal or wood. There is no right or wrong – it is a personal preference.

- Forks, spades, rakes and hoes need extra care and attention when choosing as these are the tools you will be using frequently. The best way to choose is to ask friends and neighbours what brand they are using, and see if you can try them out. The tread – the bit at the top of the blade where your foot will rest when digging – needs to be wide enough so your foot doesn't slip off. If they feel comfortable and are the right weight for you, then look for those tools in garden centres or on the Internet. Think about your height when you choose tools as the length of the shaft can vary between 70cm and 92.5cm. If the tool is too long for you, then it makes the task harder and more exhausting, while a tall person using a tool that is too short has to bend more and ends up with a damaged back.

- Two types of spade and fork are available – digging and border versions. The only difference between them is the width of the blade. Border forks and spades are slightly smaller and are more suited to digging among plants in the borders than digging a vegetable patch.

- Dutch hoes are the most popular type of hoe and are very easy to find. These hoes work by sliding beneath the soil, cutting weeds and loosening soil as you push it forward and again when you pull it backwards.

- A good soil rake will break up clods and create a smooth surface on newly dug soil, making it easier to plant seeds.

- Multi-change garden tools – if more than one person of varying heights will be using the tools, multi-change garden tools are worth considering. You buy one or two handles then add an interchangeable head such as a hoe or rake. The tool heads simply snap and lock firmly into place; releasing the heads is just like using a seatbelt. Tools with extendable handles are another popular option – you alter the height of the handle to suit your needs. The important thing to remember is to lock the handle firmly in place otherwise it can be a nasty shock when it changes height unexpectedly!

- Hand tools are needed for working when you are doing a light tidy up of beds and borders or planting bulbs and other small plants. Trowels which have measurements engraved on the blade are very useful when it come to digging holes for bulbs, while dibbers can make the tiny holes necessary for planting seeds and seedlings.

- Protect your knees – kneeling on the ground using hand tools or planting can be cold and uncomfortable, so it is worth considering protecting your knees. A few layers of newspaper or cardboard is a cheap option, but this can get messy when the wind starts blowing it around. The best option is to invest in a pair of well-fitting knee pads which can be fastened around your knees.

- Sharpening tools tend to be forgotten by many gardeners, but they are one of the most essential items in a gardener's tool kit. Used regularly, a sharpening tool makes sure that the blades of digging tools, secateurs, loppers, shears and lawnmower blades are kept sharp and effective.

- Wheelbarrows can be frustrating garden tools. Thorny material or sharp stones frequently cause punctures on pneumatic tyres and unless you are an expert at mending punctures, it can be a time-consuming task. Some wheelbarrows have solid wheels without inner tubes or valves. This enables you to avoid punctures, but they are much harder to push, especially when you have a heavy load. Wheelbarrows with polypropylene trays are more long lasting than traditional galvanised metal simply because they do not go rusty.

- Lastly, consider the importance of colour when choosing tools. Nowadays you can get tools in almost any shade of the rainbow. The number of times I have put down some green secateurs on the grass and then spent ages hunting for them are too numerous to count. A bright colour does stand out and definitely reduces frustration levels!

> 'Unless you are aiming for a pristine, bowling green style lawn, looking after a lawn requires little more than a lawnmower, trimmer and lawn rake.'

Checklist

- Check tools for length and weight.
- Make sure tools are comfortable.
- Choose a colour that will stand out.

Lawn equipment

Unless you are aiming for a pristine, bowling green style lawn, looking after a lawn requires little more than a lawnmower, trimmer and lawn rake. You can easily create drainage holes when needed by using a garden fork – so no fancy equipment needed here!

Choose your lawnmower carefully to make sure that it matches what you really need. There are five main types of lawnmower available:

- Hand driven cylinder mowers are hard work as you have to push them along in order to cut the grass, but they are very environmentally friendly as they use no power source beyond your own muscles. It can be tiring but good for the waistline!

- Rotary mowers have a horizontal blade which rotates to cut the grass. Both petrol and electric versions are available and these are very good when cutting uneven lawns, wet or long grass.

- Electric hover mowers are light to use since they hover on a cushion of air as they work, but it can be hard to mow in a straight line!

- Mulching mowers are becoming increasingly popular as they allow you to chop up the cut grass into tiny pieces which can fall back into the lawn as a natural fertiliser. Some models will act as both a mulching mower and a rotary mower, depending on which switch you use.

- Ride on mowers are only worth considering if you have a very large lawn as they are expensive, often costing over £1,000. The big advantage is that they do the job quickly.

When choosing your mower, bear in mind the size of your lawn. In general, a small lawn of less than 45m² needs a mower with a minimum cutting width of 25-30cm. A 50-185m² lawn requires a minimum cutting width of 30-35cm, while a large lawn of over 185m² needs a mower with a minimum cutting width of 35-45cm.

Whatever your choice of lawnmower, make sure that the grass catcher comes off quickly and can be carried with ease.

Trimmers are essential if you want a nice finish to the edges of the lawn. You can buy lawn edging tools which allow you to cut by hand, but this is very hard on the arms. Electric or cordless trimmers do the job faster and more efficiently, but trimmers have a cord spool which is located in the head of the trimmer and is gradually used up as you cut the grass, replacing these can be fiddly and may need a lot of patience. Again, your choice will come down to the size of your lawn.

'Whatever your choice of lawnmower, make sure that the grass catcher comes off quickly and can be carried with ease.'

Power tools

If you have hedges or lawns to care for, power tools will be needed. The big question is what to choose – cordless, electric or petrol?

Cordless tools have batteries charged from the mains electricity and possess the advantage that there are no cords to worry about, so you don't run the risk of accidentally cutting the electric cord as you work. However, when the battery has used all its power, you have to wait for it to charge up and this can take an hour or more.

Electric power tools can be very convenient. Plug them in and they can be used immediately and for as long as you need. There are disadvantages, however, and it is important to be aware of these from the beginning.

- Mains electricity can be dangerous and accidentally cutting the cord on a lawnmower or hedge trimmer can cause fatal electric shocks. You must use an RCD adaptor with every electric power tool as this will decrease the risk of shorting out your electricity if there is a problem.

- It is not a good idea to use electric tools after it is has been raining – water and electricity do not mix. Wait until plants and grass have dried before using them.

- Most electric power tools have fairly short cords – about 3m (about 12 feet). Unless you have a postage stamp sized garden, this will only reach just outside the door. Extension leads have to be used, so make sure your extension lead is long enough to go right to the bottom of the garden. Some people add extension lead to extension lead in order to get the right length, but every extension lead you add away from the mains plug actually reduces the amount of power getting through to the tool, which means you have to use even more electricity to finish the task, thus adding to the cost.

Petrol tools are generally the most expensive and are really designed for people with big gardens or professional use. They do tend to be heavier but have the advantage of being totally mobile, so you can use them anywhere in the garden.

Shredders

Shredders are a very environmentally-friendly tool and can be very useful in gardens to chop up branches, twigs, prunings, dead leaves and flowers, and hedge, shrub and rose clippings into pieces small enough to be used as a mulch around plants or added to compost. The downside is that shredders can take up a lot of space in your garage or shed and are not easy to store.

The most effective shredders have long funnels which reduce the risk of having bits of wood flying back at you as you push the garden waste into it. If it gets jammed, turn it off immediately, never try to remove obstructions unless it is turned off – the blades are incredibly sharp. Always wear goggles and gloves for protection when using a shredder.

Hiring tools

Hiring is the best option for any large piece of equipment that you are not going to use very often such as shredders, rotavators or brushcutters (very large and powerful trimmers which can be used to cut down undergrowth). Most hire shops will have a wide range of suitable equipment that can be hired for short periods at fairly low costs.

Checklist

■ Always use an RCD adaptor with any mains power tool.

■ Use as few extension leads as possible.

■ Recharge cordless tools frequently.

■ Consider hiring big tools.

Greenhouses and cloches

If you are planning to grow plants from seed, you will need a greenhouse. Traditionally, this was a big permanent wood and glass building installed in a corner of the garden, but this can pose a problem in small modern gardens where space is at a premium. Mini-greenhouses provide the perfect answer to this problem. They are more flimsy and will not last as long as a permanent greenhouse, but you can move them around the garden and even pack them away when not in use. Mini-greenhouses are made from plastic or metal and form a series of racks on which seed trays and pots can be placed, and the structure is covered with a transparent plastic cover.

Cloches are worth considering if you are just looking to protect a very small number of plants or trying to warm a small section of soil in early spring. They provide useful temporary protection against bad weather, but you do need to make sure they are well ventilated in sunshine as plants can rapidly overheat. The most useful cloches are mini-tunnels forming a selection of hoops covered with polythene or fleece which can be stretched out along a row of plants and left open or closed at the front and back.

When looking at cloches, you may also come across cold frames and it is easy to get confused between the two when you are trying to decide which product is right for you. Basically, a cloche is mobile; you can move it easily from place to place within the garden and it can come in numerous shapes, sizes and materials. Cold frames are larger, usually square or oblong and made of wood or metal with lots of glass or acrylic plastic in the structure. They are usually placed in one location and used to provide shelter for young plants, allowing plants to harden off by leaving the lid open as the days get warmer.

If you do opt for a permanent greenhouse, choose its site very carefully. You need to make sure it gets enough light all year round and isn't overshadowed by tall trees or shrubs. Most importantly, no greenhouse should be placed near a children's play area and if there is any chance of children playing in the garden at any point, replace any horticultural glass used in the greenhouse with acrylic sheeting. Horticultural glass is very thin and can easily break into very dangerous sharp pieces.

Getting to know your garden

Working out what tools you need is important, but before you get started, you need to take some time to get to know your garden. If it is an existing garden, what do you like or dislike about it? Does it meet all your needs? Are there any views you want to keep or hide?

Faced with an expanse of empty soil in a new garden, natural instinct is to fill it as quickly as possible but if you take just that little bit longer, you can make a really wonderful garden without having to continually go back and adjust it. Your garden can be much more than a grass filled plot divided by a concrete path with a few borders alongside the fences. You certainly don't have to be an expert gardener or spend lots of money to achieve this.

Think about the type of garden you would really like. What appeals to you? What do you need from the garden – somewhere for children to play safely, quick maintenance, lots of vegetables or do you need to create privacy and hide unpleasant views?

Know your soil

Knowing your soil is very important. To grow well, plants need the right type of soil. It needs to be fertile and have the right chemistry to match the plants. For example, if you try to grow rhododendrons on alkaline soil, the rhododendrons will not thrive because they need acidic soil.

A simple test kit is available from garden centres that will tell you how alkaline or acidic your soil is. If you can, try to buy a kit that will let you do more than one test as it is better to take samples from several locations.

Testing your soil

- Soil samples should be taken from about 7.5cm (3") below the surface and then allowed to dry.

- Place the soil in the test tube provided and add some water plus the chemical reagent. Shake thoroughly and allow to settle.

- After a few minutes you will see the colour of the water changing and this colour should be compared against the colour chart in the kit. If it is dark green, this means the soil is alkaline and you can grow plants like deutzia, hypericum and mock orange successfully. If the colour has changed to orange, the soil is acidic and will be suitable for rhododendrons, camellias and azaleas. A light green colour means that the soil is neutral and that most plants will be happy in this soil. For more information about the plants mentioned here, please see chapter 4.

Consider too, the type of soil involved as this can vary according to where your garden is situated in the country.

- Clay soil is heavy and slow draining. It holds water well and can be easily recognised when you pick up a handful of soil and squeeze it because it will stick together.

- Sandy soil is free draining, light and gritty. If you have this type of soil, you will need to keep adding lots of compost to keep it fertile.

- Chalky soil is pale in colour, free draining and may have chunks of chalk in it. Add plenty of compost and fertiliser to keep it in good condition.

- Peaty soil is extremely fertile and holds moisture well. It is black in colour and very crumbly to the touch.

'Your soil can be improved by adding extra materials – and it's a good idea to do this before you start planting.'

Your soil can be improved by adding extra materials – and it's a good idea to do this before you start planting. If it is chalky or sandy soil, you need to make it more moisture retentive by adding in homemade compost, manure or soil conditioners, which should be dug in before planting. If you are using manure, this should be added the autumn before planting takes place. Adding a mulch around the plants will help keep moisture in the soil.

A wet boggy soil will need to be made slightly drier if you are planning to use it for vegetable gardening and this can be done by digging in lots of compost. The best way to improve clay soils is to dig it in the winter and let the frost and winter weather break it down, then add a soil conditioning compost. Alternatively grow a green manure on the soil over the winter period and then dig it over in early spring (see page 61 for more information on green manure).

Adding homemade compost and using fertilisers such as liquid comfrey will maintain the soil fertility. For information on making your own compost, see page 34. All plants need certain minerals for healthy growth such as magnesium, copper, boron, iron, manganese and zinc. Organic fertilisers are naturally rich in these ingredients, so using them on a regular basis will ensure no problems arise. Making your own liquid comfrey is easy, plus it's a very useful and natural plant fertiliser, all you need is a comfrey plant.

- Cut some leaves off your comfrey plant and place into a plastic bag. Fasten the top securely and pierce some holes in the bottom.

- Put the bag into a container of water and leave to steep (just like a pot of tea) for about two weeks.

- Take the bag out and empty the leaves onto your compost heap. The liquid can then be diluted and used as a fertiliser.

- Dilute the comfrey fertiliser liquid (about 8 parts of water to 1 part of fertiliser), and water around the plants. You can cut comfrey leaves to make fertiliser several times a year.

If you have taken over an existing garden, have a look at the leaves on the plants to see if there are any mineral deficiencies present. The most common problems are:

- Magnesium deficiency – you can identify this if leaves turn brown and withered even though the plants are well-watered. This is common with acidic soils.

- Chlorosis – leaves turn a sickly pale yellow on alkaline soils. The problem is that there is too much lime present and this prevents the plants from getting the nutrients they need. Adding chelated iron or sequestrene will solve the problem – both of these minerals can be obtained from garden centres.

Next you need to decide what type of gardener you plan to be – organic or green? The choice is yours!

Organic gardening

Organic gardening is where only natural products and practices are used to promote fertile and healthy plants. Most gardeners follow these principles, recognising that it is better for the environment.

There are now only a few products with chemicals in such as slug pellets, paint and pesticides that can be sold to the public. Most organic gardeners won't use compost containing peat as peat is a non-renewable material.

Green gardening

This style of gardening takes organic gardening a stage further and is very popular. Green gardeners aim to conserve resources, keeping water and energy usage to a minimum. Green gardeners automatically seek natural ways of dealing with pests and assisting growth. This means you buy fewer new products and seek to reuse and recycle wherever possible.

Summing Up

■ Don't automatically opt for the cheapest tools – they may not be the most comfortable to use for long periods. Likewise, you don't need to buy the most expensive brands, so look around.

■ Make sure that all tools and equipment suit your needs – don't buy without doing your research.

■ Gardening can be dangerous, so take care. It is better to be safe than sorry. Use safety goggles, strong gloves and always use an RCD adaptor with any mains electrical tools

■ It's important to identify your soil type and prepare the soil for planting.

■ Try to follow organic and green principles and methods when gardening.

Chapter Two

Basic Design

When you watch garden programmes on the TV, there always seems to be a lot of designing, measuring and drawing up plans on graph paper before actually starting work. How much of this is actually necessary is debatable. For most people, a rough sketch on a piece of scrap paper highlighting the approximate shape of flower beds and paths is enough.

There are no hard and fast rules when it comes to designing a garden that suits you and your family. The best way to start is to list all the things that you want from the garden. For example: a lawn, flower beds, vegetables, soft fruit area, fruit trees, shed, seating area, patio, trellis or climbing plants. Don't forget the essentials like space for a washing line or compost bin. Then be realistic – how many of these features can you actually get in and what can be combined, e.g. vegetables and soft fruit, patio and seating area. Children may want a sand pit while you would like a pond – perhaps a good compromise would be to install a sand pit on the basis that it can be turned into a pond when the children are older.

Before deciding what goes where, make sure you know which are the sunny spots and the shady areas. It is no use planting shade loving plants in a sunny area, or sun loving plants in a shady area because they will not thrive. Do you prefer to sit in the shade or the sun? Remember that the angle of the sun will change throughout the year so some areas may get more sun in the summer than in spring. Use a compass to identify which way your garden faces. South facing areas will get the most sunlight all year round; north facing areas the least sunlight; east facing areas enjoy sunlight in the morning while west facing ones will be the sunniest in the afternoon and evening.

The final consideration is how exposed your garden may be. In a built up area, with gardens sheltered by neighbouring houses the wind is less of a problem but if your garden is exposed, without shelter plants and fences can be easily blown over and damaged. Check where the prevailing winds are likely to come from and add in extra shelter for vulnerable plants if necessary. Winds from the north and east are the coldest while southerly and westerly winds tend to be gentler and warmer. If your garden is very exposed, hedging is more practical than a fence as it allows some of the wind to pass through and there is less risk of it being blown down. An extra advantage is that hedging also helps deaden noise from roads.

'Long thin gardens are common in towns and on new housing estates. These can be made more interesting by breaking up into "rooms" creating a greater sense of depth as well as making it more manageable.'

Common design problems

There are two main problems that may be experienced when designing your garden but these can be easily overcome.

Long thin gardens are common in towns and on new housing estates. These can be made more interesting by breaking up into 'rooms' creating a greater sense of depth as well as making it more manageable. This can be achieved by using barriers such as a trellis, trees or tall shrubs to divide one area of the garden from another. Avoid having long straight paths in favour of winding paths to vary the layout and use lots of climbing plants to give an impression of greater width.

Boggy, wet areas are usually the result of poor drainage or the presence of naturally wet areas. Unless you want to put in new drainage systems, it is better to work with the environment and plant the area up with moisture loving plants.

Checklist

- Identify shady and sunny areas and factor this into your garden design.
- Consider how exposed your garden is.
- Look at the shape of your garden and try to maximise the proportions and make it interesting.
- Take into consideration any other features, such as boggy or wet conditions.

Marking boundaries

Fences, walls and hedges are used to mark out the boundary of your property. They provide security, privacy and identify exactly where your garden ends and neighbouring gardens begin but are frequently the cause of neighbourhood disputes. By law, you have to keep fences, walls and hedges at a height that does not affect your neighbour's right to light. If you have an existing fence, wall or hedge make sure you know who owns it as you can get into trouble for doing work on something that does not belong to you. You can trim hedges on your side, or paint fences on your side even if they do not belong to you, but if you are planning any major work like putting up a trellis or replacing a damaged section of fencing you must check ownership and get permission.

If you are a tenant you should check with your landlord the ownership of the boundary. If your landlord owns the boundary, ask for permission from them to complete any work. If the boundary is owned by someone else, you must get their permission. If you are a homeowner, check your deeds to see who is responsible for the boundary – yourself or your neighbour.

Hedging

For many years, leylandii hedges have dominated towns and housing estates. It is easy to see why – being evergreen, they provide colour in the garden all year round and create a dense, noise reducing hedge. But there is one major problem – they grow very fast. On average a leylandii hedge will grow around 1m each year, so within only a couple of years you can have a 2m hedge which requires cutting at least twice a year to maintain shape, density and acceptable height. If they grow too high, neighbours quickly become annoyed and local authorities can order a leylandii hedge to be trimmed if it is causing a nuisance.

There are more environmentally-friendly options such as yew, which makes a dense hedge and takes between six to ten years to establish itself to a reasonable height. Hawthorn is a traditional hedging material, while beech offers the advantage of keeping brown leaves all winter. A more informal hedge can be created by using tall growing rugosa roses, holly, pyracantha or berberis – these will provide summer colour as well as being effective, thorny security barriers. If you live in a rural area consider planting a traditional mixed hedge involving a variety of plants, such as hazel, blackthorn, guelder rose, beech and hawthorn.

'If you live in a rural area consider planting a traditional mixed hedge involving a variety of plants, such as hazel, blackthorn, guelder rose, beech and hawthorn.'

All hedges will require regular trimming to keep them in shape. Hedges should be planted in a single row about 30-60cm apart. Allow time for the hedge to get established by installing a simple mesh netting fence which will act as a windbreak.

Checklist

- Choose hedging materials carefully and bear in mind the length of time it takes a hedge to become established.

- Be prepared to trim regularly, especially if you have a leylandii hedge.

Paths

The shortest path is always the most direct route from A to B, but you may find that making it slightly longer will add interest to your garden, making small gardens seem much larger.

In existing gardens, it is harder to make major changes to pathways since it involves removing and resetting the materials. Unless you want to do this, it is better to concentrate on making sure the path is safe and in good condition. Check out any hollows as these will collect water – you may have to lift a few bricks and re-lay them on a new layer of sand. The other key feature to watch for is slippery areas on shady paths. This can cause nasty falls if you are not careful, and you may have to scrub the paths clean with a hard brush at regular intervals.

Materials

Creating a new garden enables you to choose the paving materials you prefer. Think about the practicalities as well as the appearance when choosing your materials.

- Concrete paving slabs are easy to install but do become slippery with algae or with ice in winter.

- Gravel is the cheapest way of covering a large area and offers no problems with ice in winter. Regular raking is needed to deter weeds but you can minimise this by laying the gravel on thick polythene sheeting.

- Block paving is popular but takes time to install as the bricks have to be individually placed in the chosen pattern.

- Bark paths made of thick layers of chippings are only suitable in back gardens. You need to top up these paths every few years as the bark degrades into the soil; it is a good option for children's play areas or for a naturalistic look in shady areas.

Bear in mind that local authority permission is now required if you are planning to lay more than 5m^2 of impermeable (i.e. doesn't allow water to pass through it) material such as concrete in front gardens. Preference is always given nowadays to the use of permeable materials such as gravel or block paving which will reduce the amount of water running off a property.

Steps

It is better to avoid steps wherever possible as accidents caused by falling down steps are all too common. A sloping path is much safer especially if it is being used by young children or elderly people – it also makes moving wheelbarrows and lawnmowers around much easier. If you have to have steps, or have existing ones, make sure that they are well lit and their location obvious. Cut back any obscuring foliage so that the steps can be clearly seen.

Lighting

Adding some lighting to a garden can make it much easier to enjoy the garden all year round. It can highlight dark corners, making it safer and more secure. Traditionally, low voltage garden lighting has involved laying cables and linking into mains electrical systems. This form of lighting is still available and has its advantages since it can be turned on and off when needed. If you are considering installing electrical lighting, the law says it must be installed by a qualified electrician.

Solar lighting is much easier to install and is very environmentally friendly. Individual lights have their own solar panel and often incorporate an on/off switch allowing the battery to charge up but not release its power until required. Running costs are minimal unless you need to replace a part or add further lights. Solar lights can be installed within minutes as all you have to do is assemble the light and push the spike into the ground. Lights should be placed in a spot where they are going to capture sunlight for much of the day. Even in winter, most solar lights will obtain enough power to provide lighting for a few hours.

Checklist

- Keep paths in good condition and remove algae as soon as it appears.

- Sloping paths are safer than steps but if you have existing steps ensure they are well lit and not hidden by plants.

- Use lighting to highlight dark areas and increase safety, or to simply enjoy your garden for all year round.

Security

We think about the security of our homes, fitting good quality locks and taking basic precautions but not many people consider the security of their gardens and this can be an expensive error. According to Home Office figures, over 5,000 gardens are targeted by thieves every week. Thousands of pounds worth of garden equipment is stolen every year, and the chances of recovering any of that property are slim. Almost anything in the garden can be stolen including plants, planters, benches, lawnmowers and tools. Even children's play equipment is not exempt – thieves stole a child's playhouse from my garden!

There are simple measures you can take that will improve the security of your garden.

- Start by fitting a strong padlock to shed doors and make sure you use it every time. Keep the keys safely in the house, not tucked under a stone nearby!

- Cover shed windows with a strong wire mesh as this makes it harder for thieves to break through the window. Also make sure that the windows cannot be easily opened from outside.

- Fit a simple alarm system to warn you if someone opens a shed door without your knowledge.

- Fit security lights that will come on automatically when anyone approaches the shed at night.

- Fit brackets into the floor or walls and use these to chain up machinery like hedge trimmers and lawnmowers.

- Take keys and batteries out of machines you are not using and store them in the house.

- Anchor garden benches into the earth. Planters should be securely fastened down or screwed to walls. Anything that makes it harder for a thief to move an item is likely to deter them.

- Keep photos and serial numbers of tools so that if the worst happens and something gets stolen, you have all the details you need at hand to claim on your insurance.

Before buying any new equipment for the garden, it is worth checking your home insurance policy as you may need to get extra insurance cover.

Call in the experts

Unless you are a really keen DIY'er, you may need to consider calling in an expert to do some jobs. Not everyone is good at putting up fences or laying paths. It may work out more cost effective to bring in an expert to do such a job than for you to spend several days trying to do a frustrating task.

There are some tasks you should always turn over to an expert. If you need to install electricity into your garden either for lighting or to run water features you must use a qualified electrician. Likewise, felling trees or cutting large hedges are best undertaken by a specialist who has access to the correct safety equipment.

Summing Up

- Think about the design of your garden – which parts get the most sun or shade? How can you make the best use of the space?

- Take care of the boundary hedges or fences, ensure you know who ownerships falls with to avoid any conflict.

- Choose the materials you want to use in your garden carefully.

- Carry out a security audit of your garden – how secure is it and how can you make it more secure?

- Use expert help for difficult tasks.

Chapter Three

Preparation

Having decided what you are going to do with your garden, the next step is to start work.

Be safe

A few things to consider before getting started in the garden:

- Make sure you're dressed comfortably in loose fitting clothes.

- During the summer, use a suitable sunscreen and reapply it regularly.

- Always wear strong shoes or boots, especially when digging as accidents can happen.

- Warm up your muscles before you start digging. Just a few stretches and massaging your calves and arm muscles will be sufficient.

- Always bend from the knees, not from your back. Knees and waists are designed for bending but your back is not. Too much bending from the back will simply result in an aching, painful back.

- Avoid digging in hot sun or when the ground is saturated as it is harder.

- Never leave tools such as garden forks lying on the ground – always place them upright in the soil.

- Use goggles to protect your eyes from flying pieces when using shredders or hedge trimmers.

- Strong gloves will help protect your hand especially when pruning thorny shrubs or from blisters when digging.

- Switch off and if necessary unplug power tools immediately after you have finished using them – it is surprising how many accidents are caused through careless use of power tools.

If this is your first time in the garden, set yourself a time limit. About 30 minutes digging is about right. Stop and have a rest or do something else for a while, then go back to digging. This will make sure you do not get exhausted and helps get your muscles accustomed to digging. After all, it is hard work!

It helps to have a goal in mind before you start. Say to yourself that you will clear a set area of soil, weed a specific flowerbed, do all the mulching or prune a tree. Aim to complete that task – anything else that you manage to get done will be a bonus. Knowing you have accomplished your goal will give you a sense of satisfaction.

Don't forget to take the basic safety precautions listed above before you start any gardening task.

Existing garden

If you have inherited an existing garden and you are not making any major changes to it, your main task will be to concentrate on removing all weeds in the flowerbeds. For small areas use a hand fork and trowel. Larger areas can be dug over with a fork. Perennial weeds such as nettles, couch grass and thistles will need to be removed completely as new plants can emerge from even the tiniest piece of root left in the soil.

If the weeds in your garden are only seedlings just use a hoe to cut through them. If it is sunny you can leave the cut up seedlings on the earth and they will just wither and die, returning nutrients into the ground. If rain is forecast, it is better to rake the weed seedlings up and place on the compost heap.

As you dig, it's good to add in some fertiliser such as chicken manure pellets or compost. This will improve the fertility of the soil and help the plants to flourish.

'If you have inherited an existing garden and you are not making any major changes to it, your main task will be to concentrate on removing all weeds in the flowerbeds.'

In the spring, add about 5cm of mulching material around the plants. This will help to prevent the plants from drying out during the summer, reduce the amount of watering you'll need to do and also help deter weed growth because the mulch prevents sunlight from reaching weed seeds which lie there in wait.

There are many different types of material you can use for mulch. The most popular are:

- Bark chippings.
- Newspaper.
- Grass clippings.
- Old carpet.
- Black polythene or weed control fabrics.
- Gravel.

Which kind of mulch you use depends on where you are using it. In flowerbeds bark chippings are the most common mulch. They are decorative, effective and will eventually decompose into the soil adding valuable nutrients.

Newspaper, black polythene or weed control fabrics need to be covered over with grass clippings, bark chippings or gravel to hold them in place and to make them more decorative.

In a vegetable plot, newspaper, black polythene, old carpets and grass clippings are the most useful. Just put some bricks or large stones to hold down newspaper or polythene. Cut up old carpet into pieces that are suitable to go round fruit bushes and trees. Make sure that any soil is brushed off the carpet otherwise weeds will take root on it.

'If you have a new garden or are taking on an allotment, this pre-planting phase will take longer. Begin by using some string to mark out the rough layout of flower beds and vegetable areas.'

New garden

If you have a new garden or are taking on an allotment, this pre-planting phase will take longer. Begin by using some string to mark out the rough layout of flower beds and vegetable areas. Adjust the layout until you have it exactly as you want it.

If your garden has had turf laid you will need to use a spade to dig up the areas you want for flower beds and vegetable patches. Place the turf upside down in a corner of the garden. Put the next layer of turf on top of the first, always making sure that the grass layer is face down. When all the turf from the new bed is removed, put an old carpet over the heap. This will encourage the turf to decompose quickly and turn into compost. If your garden does not have turf laid already then you will find more information about planting a lawn in chapter 6.

The next step is to begin digging. Start at one end of the patch and work in a straight line digging a long trench down to the other end. It should be about the depth of one spade. As you dig, put all the soil into a wheelbarrow or onto a tarpaulin. Remove any long roots from nettles, thistles or couch grass as you see them and put these to one side for disposal. When the trench is complete, put a layer of well rotted manure or compost in the base of the trench.

Dig another trench alongside the first one. As you dig, fill in the first trench with soil from the second. Continue digging layers of trenches, adding manure and filling them in with soil from the next one until you reach the end of the plot. The final trench should be filled in with soil from the very first trench that you dug. Rake over all the soil to break down any large clods of earth.

If you are preparing a flowerbed for permanent planting, it is worth considering installing a permanent mulch of black polythene or a weed control fabric. This will cut down on long-term weeding and help conserve moisture within the soil. However, bear in mind that this option only works if you have very, very carefully removed every trace of perennial weeds from the soil. Nettles and couch grass are very strong, and if any scraps of roots are left they will eventually grow and force their way through or around the barrier.

It is important to soak the soil really thoroughly before putting the mulching fabric in place and fasten it down with pegs or heavy stones. Cut a crosswise slit into the fabric to make an opening big enough to dig the soil and put a young plant in. Carefully replace the soil around the plant and firm it down. As black polythene and weed control fabrics do not look very pretty, cover all exposed areas with a thick layer of a decorative material such as bark.

Problem soil

Sometimes you may find your soil is really hard and difficult to dig by hand. If this happens, you may need to hire a rotavator from a local hire shop. A rotavator acts like a very powerful spade, cutting deeply through the earth and breaking it up. When the soil has been loosened, you will need to dig it over properly, adding manure or compost.

When using a rotavator:

▪ Check it is not too heavy for you to use.

▪ Wear strong boots and gloves.

▪ Make sure there are no electric wires, gas pipes or water pipes in the area – rotavators will chop through them!

If the soil is really poor in quality and has very little growing on it, even weeds, you will need to add lots more fertiliser and compost to get it healthy again. Pellets of chicken manure are one of the cheapest fertilisers, or you can buy soil conditioners. These just have to be sprinkled on the soil and then dug in.

Most fertilisers, including homemade compost, can be dug in and the soil used immediately. If you have added fresh horse manure, the soil needs to be left for a season. Horse manure is best dug into the soil in the autumn and left to break down over the winter period. Do not put horse manure directly around existing plants as it will be too rich for them and will cause damage.

'Pellets of chicken manure are one of the cheapest fertilisers, or you can buy soil conditioners. These just have to be sprinkled on the soil and then dug in.'

Making compost

Every garden and kitchen creates waste materials that can be turned into compost and used to add nutrients to the garden. It is a free resource reusing materials you would otherwise have thrown away. All you need is a compost bin to put it in and these can be obtained cheaply from local councils. There are four main types of compost bin – plastic, wooden, rotary and wormeries.

- Wooden compost bins – these square bins have slatted sides and can be handmade out of pallets. The compost material is placed onto the ground allowing worms to enter the heap and break down the material. Keep the heap warm all year by placing an old carpet on top. The biggest problem with this type of bin is that it does not keep out the mice and rats. Many unlucky gardeners have removed the top of the heap only to find a nest of mice inside!

- Plastic bins – this is the usual type sold by local councils and they are very good at keeping compost heaps warm but you must make sure that the lid fits tightly and cannot be blown away. When high winds are forecast it can be useful to put a couple of bricks or heavy stones on the lid to hold it down.

- Rotary bins – these bins are more expensive but they speed up the compost making process. Instead of having to dig over the heap regularly you simply have to turn a handle and rotate it three or four times a week. A good rotary bin can make useable compost within a couple of months.

- Wormeries – these are a specialist form of compost bin for kitchen waste and are only suitable if you are not squeamish about handling worms! They need to be placed close to the house in a sheltered spot. A wormery usually has three tiers of bins filled with kitchen waste and decomposing material being eaten by the worms. When the worms have finished eating all the waste in the bottom bin, they move upwards into the next bin. This leaves the compost in the bottom bin ready to be used in the garden. When it has been emptied, you put the bin at the top of the wormery and start filling with fresh waste. It can be quite a speedy process but you do need a good supply of kitchen waste on a regular basis as the worms eat up to half their body weight daily.

'Every garden and kitchen creates waste materials that can be turned into compost and used to add nutrients to the garden.'

Making a compost heap is not hard – it is just a matter of remembering which materials to use, the best things for your compost heap are:

- Uncooked vegetable peelings, salad and fruit.
- Garden waste such as grass clippings, hedge trimmings, leaves and pruned material.
- Dead indoor plants or cut flowers.
- Dead annual and container plants.
- Fresh farmyard manure.
- Twiggy material.
- Pruned woody stems.
- Shredded paper, especially newspaper.
- Cardboard egg boxes.
- Cardboard – but first remove any staples or sticky tape, then rip it into pieces before adding to the compost heap.
- Tea bags and ground coffee.
- Egg shells (break them up first).
- Wood ash.
- Hair from your hairbrush or from pet brushes.
- Straw and hay.
- Natural fabrics like cotton and wool as long as they are cut into small pieces.

There are some types of waste that should never be added to a compost heap:

- Meat and bones.
- Fish.
- Dairy products.
- Cat/dog litter.
- Large logs or pieces of wood.

- Coal ash.

- Diseased plants.

- The roots of perennial weeds like nettles or thistle.

- Weeds that have flowered and begun to seed.

- Glossy paper.

- Soot.

- Cooked food.

Adding this type of material will encourage rats and mice to scavenge for food, as well as encouraging weeds and diseases into your garden.

To make good compost, all you need is waste material, strong arms, patience and a well-organised heap. Whatever type of bin you have, you must include a selection of waste material. Just one or two types of waste material is not enough. It is best to start by building up the heap in 15cm layers. Start with a layer of twiggy material to allow air to circulate within the heap. Then add leafy material, kitchen waste and other bits and pieces like wood ash, hair and cardboard, followed by a layer of grass clippings. Then start again with layers of twigs, kitchen waste and grass clippings.

'To make good compost, all you need is waste material, strong arms, patience and a well-organised heap.'

Give it a stir from time to time, or turn it over with a spade to bring cooler materials from the sides into the centre of the heap. Rotary bins should be turned every two or three days as they are designed to make compost quickly, ideally they should be turned each day. Compost heaps left to decompose over a longer period should be turned every four to eight weeks.

When the bottom of the heap is brown and crumbly, you can remove that part of the heap and use it as a mulch or soil improver. Always remember to keep the heap warm and covered with a lid or old carpet. If the centre of the heap gets cold the materials will not break down and you will have to start again.

Compost problem solving

There are two main problems that you are likely to encounter when making a compost heap.

Compost heaps can get too wet and soggy, especially if lots of grass clippings have been added. If this happens you need to remove part of the heap and add some dry material such as twigs, newspaper or cardboard.

Alternatively, the compost heap can get too dry and this prevents the waste material from breaking down. This can be dealt with quite easily by pouring the contents of a watering can over it and adding some damp leafy material or grass cuttings. Turn over the heap with a spade to make sure that all the dry material receives some liquid. Special compost activators containing a mix of nutrients can be purchased from garden centres and watered into the heap, speeding up the composting process and decreasing the risk of the heap getting too dry.

Checklist

- Use the correct waste material for the best compost.

- Build up your compost heap in layers and turn it regularly.

- Make sure the heap does not get too wet or too dry.

- Be patient!

Weeding

This is the one task that never ends in the garden since the soil contains millions of tiny weed seeds just waiting for an opportunity to germinate. All they need is some space, light and warmth and they start to grow. Just digging over the soil will bring seeds to the surface and given the right conditions, young seedlings will emerge within a few days. Even if you install a permanent mulch of polythene or weed control fabric, weeds will try to grow in planting holes, and in any soil that settles on top of the mulch.

Fortunately if you deal with weeds quickly and regularly, they will not pose a major problem. An hour or so each week is usually enough to deal with new weed growth in most gardens.

Hoeing is the best answer on vegetable plots, around plants or exposed areas of soil. All you have to do is move the hoe backward and then forward through the weeds, cutting off the shoots and loosening the soil around their roots. Although perennial weeds will re-grow, they will be increasingly weakened and will eventually die.

In smaller areas such as underneath shrubs or among tightly packed flowers in the flower bed, hand weeding is much more effective. This avoids any risk of damaging your favourite plants or cutting them by accident! Use a hand fork or hand hoe to loosen the soil and remove the weeds.

Recognising what is a weed and what is a flower seedling can be hard for a first-time gardener. I was once told that weeds are just flowers growing in the wrong place and definitions of a weed can vary from person to person. The red flowers of corn poppies will grow rapidly wherever the earth is disturbed – some people will happily have them in the garden, while other people regard them as weeds and pull them up. Having said this, there are some plants that are almost universally accepted as undesirable elements in a garden, weeds that need to be removed and are quite easy to identify.

The most common garden weeds are:

■ Bindweed – the tiny heart shaped leaves and white or whitish pink trumpet shaped flowers look very pretty when in bloom – but for gardeners it is an absolute nightmare. As it grows, it wraps itself around plants like a parasite and a thick mass of bindweed can actually choke plants, preventing them from growing. Bindweed can grow upwards by climbing up plants and shrubs, or spread out forming a thick mat across the ground and trying to get rid of it is hard. The only practical way is to pull up all the shoots as you see them and steadily dig up the roots – but beware, the roots can go deep into the ground and spread fast to form new plants.

■ Chickweed – an annual weed which spreads rapidly by seed. It forms small plants on which stalks bearing tiny white flowers appear before producing hundreds of seeds and unfortunately, it flowers almost all year. Regular hoeing will prevent chickweed from seeding and taking root.

'Fortunately if you deal with weeds quickly and regularly, they will not pose a major problem. An hour or so each week is usually enough to deal with new weed growth in most gardens.'

Need2Know

- Couch grass – this is a perennial grass that grows up to 75cm high and is very invasive, spreading by seed as well as by strong, white creeping roots that send up new shoots at intervals. The plants are very tough and form clumps with deep roots that are hard to dig out.

- Dandelions – this is a perennial weed which has a very long tap root. Make sure that all parts of the root are dug up as it will re-grow from very small pieces. Dandelions also spread by seed from its flower heads. Remove the flowers before they begin to seed even if you are unable to dig up the root at that point.

- Docks – this is another perennial weed which has long tap roots; leave a little bit of root in the ground and it will quickly grow again. It is easily recognisable by its wide straight edged leaves and fans of reddish flowers in summer. The only advantage when you have got dock leaves growing in the garden is that you have a quick remedy available if you get stung by stinging nettles!

- Hairy bittercress – a common annual weed which has small rounded leaves and tiny white flowers with long thin seeds that explode when touched. It can grow and seed several times throughout the summer. The best way of dealing with this is to dig it up before it starts setting seed.

- Horsetail – this is a plant whose origins go back to the time of the dinosaurs and not surprisingly it is a real survivor. The roots are extremely deep and it spreads rapidly. In spring, the first signs of horsetail can be seen when tiny white or whitish brown tubular mushroom shaped growths appear above the soil. These grow into tough green stalks up to 30cm high, topped by layers of thin green fronds. Horsetail can form a thick mass of growth, choking small plants, growing through and into taller ones. Hoeing regularly in will deter weed growth, and try to dig up as many roots as possible. Later in the growing season, pull up as many of the fronds and stems that you can find.

- Nettle – there are two types of nettle, both of which are perennial weeds and will grow from just the tiniest piece of root left in the soil. It can grow up to 90cm tall with flowers in the summer. Stinging nettle has pale drooping flowers and thin hairs on all the leaves and flowers causing painful stings if you brush against it. Dead nettle has white flowers and does not sting. Digging them up is the only real answer to the problem of nettles. However, they can also be useful plants if you are planning a wild corner of the

'Nettle – there are two types of nettle, both of which are perennial weeds and will grow from just the tiniest piece of root left in the soil.'

garden. Nettles are home to many insects and cutting stems and leaves regularly provides good nutritional material for compost bins. Picking the tops of nettles (before they flower) and adding hot water makes a lovely tea, or you can boil them to make soup.

- Thistle – this is one of the most easily recognisable weeds and can be found anywhere. It is a tall growing perennial weed which has deep spreading roots. The spiky leaves and bright purple/blue spiky flowers can look very attractive but the thousands of tiny seeds it produces cause major problems. You should always wear thick gloves when cutting down or digging up thistles as the tiny thorns on the stems and leaves can be very painful.

Checklist

- Hoe or hand weed regularly to keep down the weeds.

- Use a mulch to prevent weeds growing up through the soil.

- Dig out perennial weeds.

Summing Up

- Follow the common sense garden safety tips to avoid accidents while gardening.

- Get a compost bin and make your own compost.

- Weed regularly and do not allow the weeds to grow strong.

Chapter Four

Choosing and Planting

Now your garden is ready for planting, the big decision has to be made – what plants do you choose? Faced with the thousands of plants on offer in any garden centre, it can be an intimidating prospect, especially if most of the labels are full of Latin names. It is bad enough if you have only a small area to fill within an existing garden and filling a brand new garden is even harder.

Don't panic! If you do your homework and know what you want, then the task is much easier. Have a look through a few gardening books and look at neighbouring gardens to see what types of plants you like. Decide on colour themes – do you want a hot or cool garden? Lots of reds, yellows and oranges create a bright, vibrant hot garden, while blues, purples and whites give a cooler look. If you have failing sight, opt for plants with lots of texture such as stachys, or have aromatic leaves like sage, lavender and rosemary.

Always choose plants that will suit your soil. It is much easier (and more successful) to work with your natural environment than against it. Use a soil tester to check whether your soil is alkaline or acidic (see chapter 1).

If you have an area of the garden that is always wet or muddy, consider planting a bog garden or putting in a pond rather than spending a lot of time trying to dry it out. Remember that such wet areas can provide valuable drainage during storms. One of the biggest causes of flooding is due to people filling in natural drainage areas such as ditches or ponds so when heavy rain comes, there is nowhere for it to go, leaving it to spread across the garden – or if you are really unlucky, into your house.

'If you have an area of the garden that is always wet or muddy, consider planting a bog garden or putting in a pond rather than spending a lot of time trying to dry it out.'

Small gardens need to include plants that offer more than just one season of interest in order to keep the garden looking good all year round. Good choices are evergreens and plants like dogwoods with their summer flowers and brightly coloured red or gold winter stems, shrub roses with flowers followed by hips in the autumn, choisya ternata sundance that has fragrant flowers and evergreen yellow leaves, or perovskia with lovely blue spikes of flowers and grey white stems. Another good choice is the evergreen mahonia with blue/green leaves and sweet smelling yellow flowers in spring, followed by blue berries (not the edible kind though).

A combination of trees, shrubs, roses, bulbs, perennials and annuals will create a mixed planting suitable for any garden. So what are best choices if you are looking for plants that will give fragrance, colour and interest to your garden yet are also easy to grow and require no special soil conditions or care?

'A combination of trees, shrubs, roses, bulbs, perennials and annuals will create a mixed planting suitable for any garden.'

Trees

Trees give an immediate sense of height to a new garden but you do need to choose carefully. Most trees available from garden centres are about 1.5-2m tall – but this does not reflect their ultimate height. Make an unwise choice and within a few years you could find yourself with a tree three or four times that size and requiring you to either cut it down or prune it back severely. Trees can block out a lot of light, not just in your garden but in your neighbours' and they can legally demand that a tree be cut back if the tree is affecting their right to light.

Small gardens need small trees, ideally ones that have an open canopy of leaves and branches allowing light through to the ground beneath. Worth considering are fruiting trees such as apple grown on dwarf rootstocks, ensuring they grow no more than about 3m tall. Alternatively look for silver birch, hazel, crab apples, or varieties of flowering cherry, aiming for varieties which grow to around 3.5-4.5m high.

Holly is slow growing and if you choose your variety carefully it will take a long time to become a tall tree. Worth looking for is the hedgehog holly which has variegated yellow/green leaves with lots of small spines on the leaves themselves. Another popular option is to look for trees which have a columnar shape casting very little shadow into the garden such as yew or juniper.

Need2Know

If space is very limited, it may be better to opt for tall growing shrubs like buddleia which can be cut back annually, yet will quickly grow to provide the height you require.

If you are lucky enough to have plenty of space, there is a wide range of trees available from the majestic native oaks and limes to beech and horse chestnut. These will grow tall – 30m or more!

The best time for planting trees is between autumn and early spring. This enables young trees to settle in before the dryness of summer. Although container grown trees can be planted at any time, they will need a lot of watering throughout the summer. Bare root trees are only available in the autumn and winter and should be planted immediately. If bad weather prevents you from planting a tree, you should put it in a temporary hole in soft ground. It is important to make sure that roots are protected against frost, snow and ice.

'The best time for planting trees is between autumn and early spring. This enables young trees to settle in before the dryness of summer.'

> ## Checklist
>
> - Choose trees that suit your space.
>
> - Consider the impact a tree will have on your own and your neighbours' light.
>
> - Consider using tall shrubs in small gardens.

Shrubs

Aim for the familiar and you cannot go wrong when it comes to shrubs. The majority of shrubs can be planted almost anywhere in the garden apart from deep shade. As long as they get some sunlight, they will grow quite happily.

- Buddleia (or butterfly bush as it is often known) is widely available and comes in many different colours – purple, blue, red, pink, white, yellow and orange. It grows fast and can be pruned back each year.

- Dogwoods are another good choice possessing brightly coloured red or orange stems in winter and white flowers in summer. Cut back the coloured stems in the spring and new ones will emerge ready to provide colour next winter.

- Choisya ternata is an evergreen shrub, which forms a fairly dense bush, and has orange scented flowers.

- Senecio is also an evergreen which has yellow daisy like flowers and grey foliage.

- Berberis is a dense shrub with small evergreen leaves which resemble miniature holly leaves, bright orange flowers in late spring followed by blue berries. It is ideal for all year round interest as well as providing height and an attractive background in the garden.

- Forsythia is a wonderful spring shrub as the bright yellow flowers come first followed by the leaves.

- The graceful spiraea has long sprays of white flowers on thin arching branches.

- Ribes – the flowering currant – has pretty pink, red or yellow flowers in late spring and fragrant leaves.

- Hebes provide white, blue or pink flowers throughout the summer.

- Slow growing daphnes will eventually form large bushes with bright pink flowers.

- Cytisus is an undemanding shrub with fragrant pea like flowers in red or yellow during late spring.

- Potentillas are a mainstay of almost every garden as they are covered in a mass of red, yellow, orange, pink or white flowers throughout the summer.

- Don't forget herbs like lavender, sage and rosemary as these form low growing shrubs that have lovely scented leaves as well as flowers.

For extra winter interest look for shrubs like winter jasmine with pretty yellow flowers that appear in mild spells all winter. It can form a large bush, particularly if it is given some protection from the wind by being placed against a fence or wall. Pyracantha is an evergreen with small leaves, bright orange or red berries that are much loved by small birds and white flowers in summer. Care is needed when positioning this bush in the garden as it can grow quite big and has sharp, dagger like thorns. It makes a good hedging plant as intruders are unlikely to try to push their way through pyracantha bushes but you do need strong gloves when undertaking the annual pruning in late summer.

If you want to include something just that little bit different, romneya, or the tree poppy as it is sometimes known, is a good option. You can cut it back almost to the ground every spring, feed it and then leave it to grow up to 1.5-2m tall with a stunning show of sweet smelling white poppies covering the bush from July to October. Another good alternative is the amelanchier which will eventually form a small tree possessing young copper coloured leaves, turning steadily green and ultimately yellow in autumn with small white flowers followed by red berries that turn black.

Shrubs can be planted all year round as they are only available as container grown plants.

> ### Checklist
>
> ▪ Choose shrubs with more than one season of interest for small gardens.
>
> ▪ Remember you need winter interest as well as summer.

'Shrubs can be planted all year round as they are only available as container grown plants.'

Roses

Many people regard roses as hard work, requiring lots of pruning and time spent dealing with diseases. In reality, it depends a great deal on the varieties you choose to plant. Many modern roses are bred for disease resistance and long flowering periods. Floribundas will flower throughout the summer as long as you remove all dead flowers regularly. Shrub roses are often overlooked but they can be brilliant in the garden offering lots of colour, fragrance and hips. Particularly good for hedging or filling a large space are varieties of rosa rugosa, which is a very sturdy shrub rose with red, pink or white flowers, while English roses growing to about 1.5m tall such as the rich pink Gertrude Jekyll or the yellow Graham Thomas offer the beauty and perfume of old fashioned roses with long term flowering and good health. Iceberg is a reliable white flowered floribunda but unfortunately it does not have much scent.

The best way to choose a rose is simply to go to a good garden centre when roses are in bloom and smell as many as possible. Decide which colours and scents you prefer. Shrub roses generally require little pruning beyond cutting out dead branches, while English roses and floribundas will cope with a general prune once a year removing weak branches and trimming longer stems back to a required length.

During autumn and early winter roses are available as bare root plants and these should be planted immediately. Roses can also be purchased in containers and these can be planted at any time.

'Perennials are plants that reappear each year and are the mainstay of any garden providing colour and leaves from spring to late autumn.'

Checklist

- Roses need some looking after but deadheading and pruning regularly should keep your roses tip top.

- Floribundas will flower all summer and take relatively little effort to care for.

- Choose your roses for fragrance, health and height.

Perennials

Perennials are plants that reappear each year and are the mainstay of any garden providing colour and leaves from spring to late autumn. Many of the perennials on sale nowadays are the same cottage garden plants that have been around for many years. They are easy to care for – remove dead leaves in late winter and give the new shoots a little fertiliser, then leave them to grow. Hardy geraniums, aquilegias, solidago, helianthemums, cornflowers, hemerocallis, campanula, dianthus, lupins and asters are among the most popular perennials. Stachys is a grey leaved ground cover plant often referred to as Lambs Ears, reflecting the lovely texture of the leaves and its tall white flowers.

Perennials will spread naturally and some varieties such as dianthus will provide ground cover even in winter. Perennials come in all shades of the rainbow and can be low growing such as helianthemums which grow about 30cm tall, or tall growing like campanula or lupins which can reach 1-1.5m tall. If your garden is very exposed to the wind you will probably need to provide support from stakes or grow rings for delphiniums and other tall perennials as they can be easily broken down by heavy rain or strong winds.

For winter colour it is worth including a clump of hellebores. These are lovely plants that flower from mid-winter to late spring, depending on variety, and have large saucer-shaped white, pink, green or purple flowers while the wide leaves create good ground cover. Primulas are often regarded as purely a bedding plant to be replaced after flowering, but they are also very good perennials offering an incredible range of colours. Many primulas will flower quite happily twice a year in spring and then again in autumn, while the delicate pale yellow flowers of primroses are an essential part of spring gardens.

If you want to try something just a little bit different at the back of a border, meadow rue is a lovely choice with its dainty flowers and delicate white, purple or mauve flowers. The grey/green foliage and blue spikes of the nepeta plant are a perfect choice for cat owners – cats love the aromatic foliage and will happily roll in it for ages, yet it retains a good appearance.

Container grown perennials can be planted all year round and you can also grow perennials from seed, but these generally do not flower until the following year.

Checklist

- Perennials are low maintenance – remove the dead leaves in late winter and give the new shoots a little fertiliser.

- Stake tall growing perennials so they don't get blown over.

Bulbs

No garden can be without a few bulbs. They are most popular in late winter/ early spring when you can have a display taking in turn snowdrops, aconite, crocuses, grape hyacinths, daffodils, bluebells, hyacinths and tulips, but there are bulbs for other times of the year as well. Worth considering for summer use are montbretia which has sword-like orange or red flowers in July and August, or freesias, irises and lilies, while for later in the year there are autumn flowering crocuses and the half-metre tall pink nerine flowers.

Bulbs can be used throughout the garden, with spring bulbs ideal for naturalising under trees and tall growing shrubs where they can benefit from the shade in summer.

Spring flowering bulbs can be planted during late summer to early winter. Summer, autumn and winter flowering bulbs should be planted during late spring to late summer. Buy bulbs as early as possible in the season from garden centres, and plant immediately. You need to look for plump bulbs that are hard and are not dried out.

'Spring flowering bulbs can be planted during late summer to early winter. Summer, autumn and winter flowering bulbs should be planted during late spring to late summer.'

Checklist

- Choose only healthy bulbs at the garden centre.
- Plant a wide mix for spring colour.

Annuals

There are two types of annuals: bi-annuals and annuals. Bi-annuals take two years to flower. In the first year they form clumps of leaves, then in the second year they flower, create seeds and die. Typical bi-annuals include wallflowers and mullein. Annuals are exactly that – they grow, flower, seed and die all within the same year. Some are hardier than others and can cope with light frosts, but the majority should not be planted out until all danger from frost has ended. Typical of this type of plant are marigolds, tagetes, ageratum and petunias.

Annuals are brilliant for filling in gaps among permanent plants and can be grown quickly and easily from seed. Good, easy to grow varieties are centaurea, poached egg plant, Virginia stock and night scented stock. All will grow quickly and provide ground cover in a new garden. Take care to remove all dead flower heads as this will encourage the plants to keep growing and flowering for a much longer period.

Dead annual and bi-annual plants should be pulled up and placed on the compost heap.

Checklist

- Do not plant annuals outside until frosts are over.
- Make sure you know which type of annual you are planting.
- Dead head your annuals regularly to encourage flowering.

Climbers

Choose climbers with great care – bear in mind the amount of space they need to fill. Most climbers will grow fast and can easily grow taller than expected. You can get both perennial and annual climbers. Perennial climbers include plants like honeysuckle, jasmine, roses, wisteria, ivy and clematis, while typical annuals include sweetpeas and thunbergia. For something slightly different you could try the climbing hydrangea. This is ideal for a shady wall and can take a year or two to get settled. Ultimately it can grow into a very large plant covering up to 20m of space possessing glossy leaves with white flowers at mid summer.

One climber which is best avoided unless you have a really big space to fill is the Russian vine. This is often described as the mile a minute plant because it really grows fast – at least 4m every year and can form quite a heavy plant. There are masses of white flowers all summer and the plant can be cut back in winter ready for new growth when spring comes.

'Annuals are brilliant for filling in gaps among permanent plants and can be grown quickly and easily from seed.'

Container grown climbers can be planted all year round. Annual climbers such as sweet peas or black eyed Susan can be grown from seed and should be planted out as soon as the risk of frost has ended.

> ## Checklist
>
> ■ Choose your climbers with care, make sure you have the space and don't let it grow out of control.

Handle with care

If you have young children choose your plants carefully. Avoid planting thorny plants such as holly, rose and pyracantha close to children's play areas. It is important to remember that some plants are poisonous and are better avoided until children are at an age when they can learn what they can and cannot touch or eat around a garden. However, don't be too alarmed if you already have mature shrubs with lots of berries in the garden, just remember to take a little extra care by removing all berries or seeds within touching distance. You can also find that some plants may irritate your skin. So what are the key plants that pose potential dangers in the garden?

■ Rue contains a sap that can cause a serious reaction in some people. In addition the soft grey leaves can cause redness, itching and blistering of the skin in sunny weather.

■ Monkshood is a beautiful blue flower but all parts of the plant contain poisons that can be fatal if eaten or absorbed through the skin.

■ All parts of spurge laurel are toxic and should be avoided.

■ Laburnum is a very attractive tree possessing delicate branches and yellow flowers but the seeds, twigs and leaves are poisonous.

■ Lupin seeds and leaves are poisonous.

■ Pyracantha and yew have berries which are poisonous if eaten.

■ Wisteria is a lovely purple flowered climber but all parts of the plant can cause harm if eaten.

- Primulas may cause skin rashes and itching as can the umbrella tree and the California glory plant.

- Dieffenbachia, also known as the dumb cane or leopard lily poses major hazards. Touching the sap can cause rashes, while if any part of the plant is eaten it can cause the mouth, tongue and throat to swell and cause breathing difficulties.

- Pampas grass and yucca have needle sharp leaves that can cut hands easily.

Checklist

- Bear in mind there are possible allergic reactions to plants if you are taking over an established garden.

- Consider possible dangers for children and try to remove low-hanging berries so they can't be eaten.

Planting

This is one of the most enjoyable garden activities as you can suddenly see the results of all your hard work. It is a lovely feeling to see a formerly bare plot newly full of plants, bringing the garden alive. Even just planting one or two extra shrubs or flowers in a corner of an existing garden will make a difference to its overall appearance. Container grown plants can be planted at any time, but seeds and bulbs can only be planted at specific times of the year, usually spring or autumn.

Begin by collecting up everything you need – plants, fork and spade, hand tools for small plants, fertiliser, watering can and if necessary stakes and ties for trees.

Planting container-grown plants

- If you want to plant something that has been grown in a container you should start by digging a hole the same depth as the container, but slightly wider.

'Container grown plants can be planted at any time, but seeds and bulbs can only be planted at specific times of the year, usually spring or autumn.'

- Put some water and a small handful of fertiliser in the bottom of the hole to give the new plant some instant food as it settles into its new spot.

- Pour some water over the plant before trying to remove it from its pot – this will make the task easier. Then, gently ease the plant out by squeezing the pot sides and loosening any roots that are growing out of the bottom. Put your hands on the top of the compost and around the base of the plant and carefully tip the pot over so that the plant falls onto your hand.

- The next step is to check the plant roots. If they are growing in circles around the root ball, the plant is becoming root bound. You can deal with this by easing out the strong main roots so that they are encouraged to grow outwards into the soil.

- Then put the plant into the hole and fill it in, firming down the soil by stepping on it and then water thoroughly.

If the plant is a tree or tall shrub, you will need a stake to prevent the plant being blown over by high winds. So before you fill in the hole, put a stake next to the root ball, but not through the roots. This is a two person task as one person needs to hold the stake upright while the other one fills in the hole. The plant should be fastened to the stake with a plant tie, don't use string or wire as they cut into the stem of the plant.

Planting bedding plants

Bedding plants come in trays of a dozen or more plants from the garden centre. If you buy them early in the season, you will need to harden them off before you plant them in the garden so they become accustomed to the change in climate, particularly night time temperatures. If you plant them out immediately, you may find that the plants will die or experience difficulty in settling into your garden.

- Keep the trays under cover at night, and put them outside for steadily increasing periods of time during the day, before decreasing the amount of protection you give them at night. When they can be left safely outside all the time you can plant them in the garden.

- Once they're ready to be planted in the garden, follow the same instructions as for container-grown plants, taking extra care as they will be small.

Take extra care with annuals such as marigolds and lobelia since these will often be available for purchase cheaply as very young plants in late spring, but you cannot plant them outside until all danger from frosts have passed. You will need to keep them undercover for much longer and may have to put them into larger pots for a while.

Planting seeds outside

Growing plants from seed is not difficult and can be a very inexpensive way of providing plants for the garden. New gardeners should always look for packets containing easy to grow seeds. The packets will indicate when the best time for planting will be and whether they can be planted straight into the soil, or have to be started off in trays under cover.

If you are planting seeds straight into the soil it is a good idea to mark out your planting area with a little sand or string and have a label prepared. There is nothing more irritating than forgetting where you planted seeds and accidentally digging them up! Avoid windy days if you are planting small seeds as they are likely to be blown away as fast as you plant them.

'Growing plants from seed is not difficult and can be a very inexpensive way of providing plants for the garden.'

- Make sure the area of soil is free from weeds and rake over the surface to create a nice smooth surface free of any large stones or clods of earth.

- Next cover the soil temporarily with a layer of fleece or polythene to warm it up, fasten the covering down with some heavy stones or pieces of wood to stop it from blowing away.

- Carefully sprinkle the seeds on the ground and cover with a thin layer of soil before gently watering in and leaving to grow. If you plant the seeds in rows across the allotted space, it is much easier to spot weed seedlings as they grow.

- Check on your seedlings regularly, any weeds need to be removed quickly as they will take valuable nutrients and water away from the flowers you are seeking to grow.

Planting seeds into pots or trays

Planting seeds into pots or trays requires a little more care and attention but it is not hard to do. All you need are some suitable containers, even yoghurt pots or foil trays with drainage holes pushed in will serve the purpose. Pots are best for large seeds and trays are best for small seeds.

- Fill your containers three-quarters full with a compost designed for use with seeds and seedlings.

- Spread the seeds evenly across the compost and aim to keep as much space as possible between the seeds.

- Then cover with a thin layer of compost, give the seeds some water and put a label in the container.

Most seeds can then be left in a light place under cover such as in a mini greenhouse, under a cloche or even left on a window sill to grow. Sometimes the packet will state that the seeds should be covered over and left in a dark, warm place until germination has taken place. In those circumstances put the pots or tray in a transparent plastic bag, fasten it with a rubber band to keep the moisture in, and then place the container in the base of an airing cupboard. Keep watch over them on a daily basis and when the first shoots start appearing, take the container out of the bag and place it in a warm place to harden off before moving the container to a greenhouse.

You will probably need to move the young plants into larger pots before they are ready to go outside in the garden. It is easy to tell when this is necessary – roots start appearing out of the bottom of the pot or tray and the plants look crowded.

- First get some pots ready, three quarters full of compost and a little plant food then thoroughly water the container of young seedlings.

- Working from the edge of the tray inwards, carefully take out one plant at a time. Do not touch the stems as these will break easily. Instead, hold them gently by the leaves and ease them out of the tray using a pencil to loosen the roots.

- Put the young plant straight into its new pot and firm some soil around it. Give it some water and put it in a shady spot for a while to settle down.

Planting bulbs

Bulbs should always be planted in groups of at least three or four bulbs. Small bulbs like crocuses, snowdrops, bluebells and aconite can be planted together in the same hole as long as you space them out on the soil. Larger bulbs like daffodils, tulips and hyacinths need separate holes.

- Check the planting depth on the packet and dig a hole according to the instructions. This is important because if the bulbs are planted too near the surface, they will send up leaves but no flowers.

- Put a little bit of compost and some water in the bottom of the hole ready for planting.

- Make sure you plant the bulbs the right way up, bulbs have 'necks' at the top and often there are dry roots at the bottom.

- Cover the bulbs over with soil and water.

Checklist

- Make sure you stake tall container-grown plants when you plant them out so they don't get damaged in the wind.

- Harden off bedding plants and wait until the frosts have ended before planting out.

- Look for easy to grow seeds in your local garden centre.

- When planting seeds out mark the area and check for weeds regularly.

- Don't plant seeds on windy days as most of them will blow away.

- Make sure you follow the instructions when planting seed trays: some need light areas and some need dark areas.

- When repotting your seedlings, hold them by the top leaves not the stems so they don't break.

- Make sure you plant bulbs to the right depth, check the packets for instructions.

'Bulbs should always be planted in groups of at least three or four bulbs. Small bulbs like crocuses, snowdrops, bluebells and aconite can be planted together in the same hole as long as you space them out on the soil.'

Summing Up

- Choose plants carefully to match your garden requirements.

- Make sure you know whether your soil is alkaline or acidic.

- Bear in mind that some plants may pose health risks but as long as you take care, problems will be minimal.

- Perennials will give texture, colour and long periods of interest.

- Combine as many different types of plant as possible in your garden – shrubs, perennials and bulbs.

Chapter Five

Vegetables, Fruit and Herbs

Growing your own vegetables is becoming extremely popular nowadays and it is easy to see why. It is not difficult and even the smallest of gardens can provide a good supply of fruit and vegetables. Nothing tastes better than fruit and vegetables you can pick just before cooking, your know that there will be no residues of pesticides or sprays – and you know that it is reducing your food bills.

Setting up a food growing area

Having decided that you are going to grow some of your own food, the first thing is to decide how much space you can use for the purpose. Traditionally this has meant devoting an area of the garden to long rows of vegetables and a few fruit bushes, raspberry canes and fruit trees. Most modern gardens do not have the space for this type of gardening. In winter it can look extremely bare and uninviting and if you only have a small plot then your garden can look very boring for part of the year.

There are alternatives, for example, increasing numbers of gardeners are opting to create raised beds. These beds can be either totally raised on a platform several feet high suitable for gardening by people in wheelchairs or are

'Nothing tastes better than fruit and vegetables you can pick just before cooking, your know that there will be no residues of pesticides or sprays – and you know that it is reducing your food bills.'

edged by planks of wood one to two feet high. The advantage to this method is that you can clearly identify which plants have been planted in which bed, and it also provides a way of deterring carrot fly from attacking the produce.

Some people opt for a potager style garden where you can divide the garden into beds using brick or gravel pathways. The beds may be edged formally using box (an evergreen shrub), step over cordon fruit trees or a relaxed edging of nasturtiums, violas, pinks and herbs. The interior of the beds is then filled with fruit, vegetables, herbs and annual flowers.

'Applying fertilisers regularly is very important to ensure the long term productivity of your new vegetable plot. Each time you harvest a crop, it has taken nutrients out of the soil and these need to be replaced.'

Mixed gardens in which fruit, vegetables and herbs are placed in gaps within an established garden border are increasingly common. It is a style of gardening that is suitable for modern gardens making them very flexible and versatile. The key to success in making this type of garden work is to make sure that every bit of space is filled all the time. As soon as one crop is ready for harvesting, it is taken out and fertiliser added to the soil before a new, different crop is planted.

If you are aiming for a mixed garden you should choose productive crops that also look decorative such as curly leaved lettuce, bright red and yellow stemmed chard or the feathery leaves of fennel and carrots. Gooseberry and blackberry bushes can be slipped in among larger bushes at the back of the borders. Remember too that trellises and archways can often support a decorative flower such as a clematis as well as fruit like raspberries and Oregon thornless blackberries that offer good autumn colour.

Whatever style of vegetable garden you choose, always take care to make sure you have easy access to the produce without having to tread on other plants.

Fertilisers

Applying fertilisers regularly is very important to ensure the long term productivity of your new vegetable plot. Each time you harvest a crop, it has taken nutrients out of the soil and these need to be replaced. There are two types of fertiliser available and choosing between them depends on whether you are planning to be an organic or inorganic gardener.

Organic

These are natural products of plant or animal origin, which break down naturally into the soil, for example:

- Manure – this is a very strong fertiliser and should be dug into the soil each autumn. Alternatively mix it into the compost heap and leave it to decompose. It is quite easy to obtain if you know anyone with a horse (they will have lots to get rid of!), or ask at riding schools and farms. Garden centres sell containers of chicken manure, usually in pellet form, and this just has to be sprinkled on the soil and dug in.

- Mushroom compost – this can be obtained from any mushroom farm as it comprises compost used for growing mushrooms. It makes a wonderful soil conditioner especially if you have acidic soil as it is very alkaline in content.

- Leaf mould – if you have trees and shrubs in your garden you are going to get a good supply of free leaves every autumn. All you have to do is gather them up and put them in a container to rot down. You can make suitable containers by buying some wire netting and a few stakes – place the stakes in a rough circle or square and then wrap the netting around the outside. Alternatively you can fill strong dark plastic bags with the leaves and tie the tops tightly. Don't forget to pierce some holes in the bottom of the bags to provide drainage. The leaves will slowly rot down to make a fine, crumbly very rich nutritious mixture.

- Green manures – growing a green manure is a very natural way of adding organic materials to the soil. It can only be used on bare patches of land, for example vegetable areas during winter time by sowing the seeds of red clover, alfalfa, field beans, winter tares or mustard in the autumn. The plants grow all winter suppressing weeds and providing cover for beetles and other pest eating insects. The roots improve the soil structure and stop nutrients leaching away during winter rains. At the start of spring, before the crop starts to flower, you dig it into the ground and leave everything to decay before you begin planting your vegetables.

Inorganic

These are minerals such as ground chalk or have been manufactured from various chemical mixtures. If you are using these type of fertilisers you have to spread the minerals on the soil and dig them in, while liquid feeds have to be used every two weeks during the spring and summer.

If you are growing crops in pots and containers, it is very important to make sure they are fed regularly. They quickly use up all the nutrients in the planting material and if left unfed, they starve, creating leggy unhealthy plants that are susceptible to disease and pest attacks. The best way to feed container plants is to use slow release pellets in the planting mix or to use liquid fertilisers on a regular basis.

Checklist

- Choose your style of vegetable plot – traditional, raised beds, potager or mixed garden.

- Always apply fertilisers before planting, choose the most effective type of fertiliser for your garden and circumstances.

- Remember to feed containers every two or three weeks.

Choosing crops

Vegetables are grown from seeds or bulbs, with seeds being the most common.

- Onions and garlic are usually grown from bulbs (or cloves as they are sometimes known).

- Potatoes are grown from seed potatoes, also known as tubers. Both organic and non-organic seeds and bulbs can be obtained.

- Take great care when buying sweet corn seed from non-organic suppliers since it is frequently coated with preservatives and fungicides – hands should be washed very carefully after touching them.

Many garden centres and seed companies sell a range of plug plants in early spring. These are young seedlings that you have to grow on yourself by planting them into bigger pots and getting them accustomed to the temperatures outside before planting in the garden. They cost more than a packet of seeds but if you only want one or two plants of a specific type such as tomatoes or courgettes this can be a very cost effective way of buying them.

You can also get perennial crops like rhubarb and asparagus that appear year after year. After planting, rhubarb should be harvested very lightly for the first year, while asparagus takes two years to get settled. After this period, as long as you give the plants a good feed every year, they will regularly produce a good crop. Bear in mind that once planted, perennial crops should not be moved.

The majority of crops are easy to grow and even complete beginners can obtain a reasonable harvest. Well-known vegetables like carrots, turnips, beetroot, spinach, lettuce, peas, beans, courgettes, tomatoes and onions require very little skill as long as you plant the seeds or seedlings at the right depth and keep them well-watered and fed. If you want to try something a little different it is worth considering Jerusalem artichokes, garlic, Swiss chard, mangetout, asparagus peas or oriental vegetables such as pak choi.

It is best to choose a variety of vegetables and grow a small selection of different types. This will avoid the risk of getting massive gluts of just one or two vegetables at harvest time. A mix of root crops, peas or beans, leafy vegetables and salad vegetables works well.

- Root crops are vegetables that have their edible sections growing below the ground such as potatoes, parsnips, carrots and Jerusalem artichokes. Potatoes can be a bit tricky as they do require a lot of care. You need to buy tubers in late winter/early spring and spread them on trays or place in old egg boxes with the eyes upwards in a light yet cool and dry place. Over the next two or three weeks, the tubers will start developing long shoots. When the shoots have appeared, you can then plant the tubers outside in the garden. They need to be placed at least a spade's depth into the ground and when the leaves start appearing, you must use a spade or hoe to pull up the earth around the stems. As the plant grows taller, keep repeating this exercise as it encourages the plant to develop lots of individual potatoes and protects the new potatoes from growing too close to the surface and turning green and inedible.

'It is best to choose a variety of vegetables and grow a small selection of different types. This will avoid the risk of getting massive gluts of just one or two vegetables at harvest time.'

- Leafy vegetables are crops which are grown for their leaves and sometimes have roots or bulbs which grow close to or on the surface such as onions, spinach, turnips and beetroot. These may be available as plug plants, as seeds or as bulbs. Once in the ground, they require very little care beyond watering, feeding and dealing with any pests or diseases that occur.

- Beans and peas are sometimes referred to as legumes. Although there are bushy and low growing varieties available, the majority of beans and peas grow tall and need support. They are easy to grow from seed but make sure you cover the area with netting as mice will dig up and eat the seeds. Runner beans and French beans should not be planted outside until mid-May at the earliest as they can be killed by frost. If frosts are forecast after planting, cover the plants with a cloche or fleece to give some protection. Plant the beans around pre-erected supports such as canes tied into a wigwam shape. No more than three seeds should be planted around each cane and as they grow, tie in the stems to the supports so that they are encouraged to go in the direction you want them to grow. After that they will grow and wind around the supports.

- Salad vegetables are crops grown for their leaves and include lettuce, chard, rocket, mizuna, nasturtiums. Lettuce can be left to grow into hearts or you can cut the leaves two or three times to provide young, tender leaves for the plate. Care has to be taken to make sure that crops are harvested regularly as these plants become inedible once they start to flower. The only exception to this rule is nasturtiums as you can continue picking leaves all summer even when they are flower.

Checklist

- Aim for a mix of root crops, leafy vegetables, salads, peas and beans.

- Only plant what you will need to avoid gluts of certain vegetables at harvest time.

- Wash your hands after planting seeds treated with fungicides and preservatives.

Crop rotation

Rotating crops is essential for successful vegetable growing without having to use chemicals to correct nutritional deficiencies in the soil, or face the prospect of dealing with lots of diseases. It works on the basis that pests and diseases tend to attack related crops so by moving crops each year, you disrupt their life cycle and numbers do not build up sufficiently to create problems in future years. Another reason for following a programme of crop rotation is that crops root at different depths and take varying amounts of nutrients from the soil. Rotating the crops provides an efficient use of soil nutrients. For example, one year you grow beans in one spot and follow this the following year by growing leafy vegetables like cabbage and spinach; the leafy vegetables will benefit because bean roots fix nitrogen into the soil and break down other nutrients required to feed leafy vegetables.

Introducing a system of crop rotation is easy, especially if you are working on a raised bed system. For a three year rotation plan, draw up a plan of your vegetable area and divide it into three sections. Colour each section a different colour to make them stand out and label them A, B, and C.

'Rotating crops is essential for successful vegetable growing without having to use chemicals to correct nutritional deficiencies in the soil, or face the prospect of dealing with lots of diseases.'

	First year	Second year	Third year	Fourth year
Area A	Peas, beans, celery, onions, leeks, lettuce, spinach, sweet corn, tomatoes and courgettes.	Brussels sprouts, cabbages, cauliflowers, broccoli, turnips and radishes.	Root crops like potatoes, parsnips, carrots and beetroot.	Back to the area where each crop was originally planted in the first year.
Area B	Brussels sprouts, cabbages, cauliflowers, broccoli, turnips and radishes.	Root crops like potatoes, parsnips, carrots and beetroot.	Peas, beans, celery, onions, leeks, lettuce, spinach, sweet corn, tomatoes and courgettes.	
Area C	Root crops like potatoes, parsnips, carrots and beetroot.	Peas, beans, celery, onions, leeks, lettuce, spinach, sweet corn, tomatoes and courgettes.	Brussels sprouts, cabbages, cauliflowers, broccoli, turnips and radishes.	

Harvesting

Beans and peas need to be picked regularly as the more you pick, the more pods will appear. Take care not to damage the stem of the plant when you twist the pods off as if a stem breaks, it will stop producing pods. Leafy vegetables such as lettuce need to be picked frequently otherwise they develop long stems and flowers making the leaves bitter and uneatable. Onions, garlic and shallots should be dug up and left on the ground in the sunlight for a few days to allow them to dry off.

In some cases, you do not have to harvest all the crops at the same time. Jerusalem artichokes, parsnips, leeks and swedes can be left in the ground until you are ready to eat them. Cover them with straw or cardboard to prevent the soil around them from freezing and making it hard to dig when you need to.

'No garden can be without a few herbs. They are useful plants that can be grown in the flower beds just as well as in the vegetable plot.'

Checklist

- Rotate your crops each year to ensure healthy soil.
- Harvest your veggies regularly.

Herbs

No garden can be without a few herbs. They are useful plants that can be grown in the flower beds just as well as in the vegetable plot. Herbs do need a sunny spot to grow successfully. The most popular herbs are the most well-known ones – mint, rosemary, thyme, sage, coriander and lemon balm, while for something slightly different lovage is an easy to grow herb providing tasty stems and leaves that can be eaten as salad throughout spring and summer. If you are planning to grow mint, it's important to remember that it is a very invasive plant. It's roots will spread rapidly sending up lots of new plants and can quickly outgrow its allotted space. Fortunately mint will grow well in pots and you can also dig up chunks of plant to put elsewhere or give away. Mint is always a welcome gift, especially if you are growing some of the more unusual varieties such as chocolate mint, orange mint or pineapple.

Herbs do grow fast so you can pick them as often as you like until they start flowering, the leaves can be used in cooking, teas or used to flavour vinegar. If you are planning to dry herbs for winter use, it is best to cut long stems on a sunny day ideally in the afternoon when the oils in the leaves are at their strongest. The stems can be tied together and hung up to dry, or you can spread them on a baking sheet and place in the oven on a low heat for a short time to dry. As soon as the leaves crumble in your fingers you need to put them in a container. They will keep for several months.

If you are planning on growing your herbs on a windowsill indoors you can plant the seeds at any time during the year. If the plants are for use in the garden, it is best to plant the seeds late winter or early spring so they're ready for planting outside when the risk of frost has ended.

Plants from the garden centre can be planted straight into the garden as long as they have been hardened off. Check with the garden centre. Plug plants will normally have to be grown on at home for several weeks before planting out.

Fruit bushes

No vegetable garden would be complete with at least one or two fruit bushes. They will grow well in any soil, and as long as you cut out any dead wood, they will keep going for years. Although familiar crops like strawberries, raspberries, gooseberries, blackberries and blackcurrants are the most commonly grown, you could try fruits that are rarely available in the supermarkets such as Japanese wineberries, Jostaberry, redcurrants and white currants. These are just as easy to grow and give good harvests of succulent, tasty fruit ideal for cooking or eating raw for dessert.

Blueberries are something really special but you have to take great care with them. They can only be grown in acidic soil or in pots filled with an acidic (ericaceous) compost. Blueberries will grow to around 1.5m and the berries can be harvested when they have begun to soften and gone blue for several days. Birds find them really tasty, so you do need to cover the plants with netting when harvest time approaches.

'No vegetable garden would be complete with at least one or two fruit bushes. They will grow well in any soil, and as long as you cut out any dead wood, they will keep going for years.'

Fruit bushes come as small bushes ready for planting and the best time for planting is in the autumn or early winter. However, they can be planted at any time but will need a lot of watering during the summer.

Strawberries

'Fruit bushes come as small bushes ready for planting and the best time for planting is in the autumn or early winter. However, they can be planted at any time but will need a lot of watering during the summer.'

There are two main types of strawberries; wild or alpine strawberries, which are small and very sweet, and cultivated varieties such as the large strawberries sold in supermarkets. There are many different types: early, main crop, late and perpetual, depending on the time the fruit is picked and by planting a variety of plants you can grow fresh strawberries throughout the summer. Perpetual strawberries are particularly useful since they provide two harvests, one in June and a smaller one in the autumn. Strawberry plants should be kept for three years after which they need replacing. This can be done by potting up the small offshoots that appear after fruiting has ended. When the offshoots have developed roots, they can be planted into the ground. If replanting an area, add plenty of fertiliser and put the new plants in a slightly different spot to the original ones.

Other berries

Raspberries, blackberries and hybrid berries like Jostaberry grow tall and require strong supports. They are perennial plants which means they will continue growing year after year and will also send up lots of new shoots from the roots. These offshoots can be dug up and planted elsewhere or given away to friends. New shoots must be tied to the supports each year and all the old shoots that have borne fruit trimmed down to the ground each autumn. A small harvest will be possible in the first year after planting.

Gooseberries, blackberries, redcurrants and white currants are all berry fruits which grow on bushes. Care is required when dealing with gooseberries as these have quite sharp thorns. All the bushes will provide a harvest each year and need pruning regularly.

Fruit trees

Apples, pears and cherries are the usual tree fruits planted in most gardens but you can also get plums and apricots. Take care when choosing fruit trees as more than one tree may be required to ensure pollination (fertilisation). If there are no other similar fruit trees growing in adjacent gardens, and you have limited space, look out for family trees which have two or three complementary varieties grafted onto one rootstock such as Charles Ross, Grenadier and Worcester Pearmain apples or Conference, Doyenne du Comice and Bon Chretien pears. Remember that fruit trees do not have to be standalone varieties – you can train them against walls, as step over cordons along flower beds, or even as compact columns. If you are considering this style of fruit tree, you will have to prune carefully each year to make sure they stay in the same shape.

Fan shapes are most frequently used for cherries and plums. The branches are spread out against a wall in the shape of a fan and are tied to wires. The trees will spread 3m or more along the supports.

'Apples, pears and cherries are the usual tree fruits planted in most gardens but you can also get plums and apricots.'

Summing Up

■ Set up a food growing area in a way that suits your space.

■ Use a good fertiliser to ensure the productivity of your garden.

■ Choose a good range of plants and follow a programme of crop rotation to ensure healthy soil and crops.

■ Harvest regularly.

■ Grow invasive herbs in pots and don't harvest once they have flowered.

■ Plant fruit trees that have the correct pollination partners.

Chapter Six

Lawn Care

A grassy green space is a key element of almost every garden, especially if you have children or pets. It is a place to run and play in, or to sit and relax in comfort. Much depends on what you want – a beautiful, well cared, manicured lawn will take more time to maintain than a family lawn in which you accept that there will be some weeds or rough patches. Formal, well-cared for lawns require a lot of work removing all weeds, levelling out bumps and cutting to precise lengths.

Traditionally, most lawns were cut once or even twice a week to keep the grass as low as possible making it a very time consuming chore. With the changing climate, views have begun to change as when there is a drought or a long dry spell in summer, short lawns are the first to suffer, becoming brown deserts. As a result, it is increasingly being accepted that it is better to cut lawns less often, and leave the grass higher as this helps maintain a green appearance for longer.

Basic lawn care involves a programme of regular mowing, feeding, aerating and scarifying.

- Mowing – you should mow your lawn regularly. The frequency of mowing required depends on the type of lawn you want. If you want a fine lawn, you need to mow it two or three times a week. A standard family lawn should be mowed once a week during the growing season, except in very dry weather when the lawn should not be mowed at all. If the lawn is shady, it should be cut less frequently than a sunny lawn.

> 'Basic lawn care involves a programme of regular mowing, feeding, aerating and scarifying.'

- Feeding – apply some lawn food every spring across the surface of the lawn and this will ensure that it has all the nutrients it needs to survive the summer and recover if necessary from any drought.

- Aerating – this should be done each spring to improve the overall appearance of the lawn. Use a garden fork to push holes into the compacted lawn soil, this makes holes through which air, water and food can pass to the grass roots. Then brush in a little sand to help water to continue to permeate through the soil.

- Scarifying – this should also be done each spring. Drag a rake across the surface of your lawn removing any moss and dead grass (known as thatch) which can then be put on the compost heap. Finally use a hand trowel to dig up any lawn weeds that appear such as dandelions and add a small amount of grass seed as you fill in the hole.

New lawns

If you need to lay a new lawn, you have a choice between buying turf or seeds. Seed is the cheapest but does take longer to establish, and can lead to patchy lawns with gaps where more seed has to be sown.

Grass seed can be easily obtained at any garden centre but choose carefully to make sure that the seed mix will provide the type of grass you need as some mixes are better for hard wearing family lawns than a fine, rarely used lawn. Having dug over the soil and prepared it for planting, you will need to sow the seed at a rate of two handfuls of seed for every square metre. Rake the seed into the soil and then cover with a layer of thin mesh to protect it from hungry birds. Do not walk on the new lawn until you can see the grass growing, and don't cut it until it is at least 5cm tall.

Turf lawns can be installed within a matter of hours. Time is very important because it is essential that the pieces of turf do not dry out. The first thing to do is mark out the shape of the lawn and dig it over lightly, removing any perennial weeds. Walk over the soil to firm it down and lightly rake over to create a level surface. Then starting from one side of the lawn lay rows of turf onto the soil

'Turf lawns can be installed within a matter of hours. Time is very important because it is essential that the pieces of turf do not dry out.'

Need2Know

until the area is completely filled. Knock the edges of the turf into place using the back of a rake. The earlier the lawn is walked on the better, as it helps firm down the turf and prevents weeds growing underneath.

Checklist

- Don't mow your lawn too often in order to keep the grass nice and green through dry periods.

- Follow the basic lawn care steps to keep your lawn healthy each year. Have some grass seed available to fill in gaps that appear after scarifying.

- If you need to lay a new lawn you must choose between seed or turf.

Common lawn problems

No lawn is trouble free but it is easy to identify and deal with the most common problems.

Anthills

Ants usually cause a slightly raised area of earth within the lawn on which grass has difficulty growing. Apart from making the lawn look untidy, ants can cause nasty bites, and if they have developed wings they can quickly create new colonies throughout the garden and even in the house. The only practical way to deal with them is to dig up the anthill. Birds will love the tasty meal presented by the insects or alternatively you can soak the area with water and drown the ants. When all the ants have gone, you will need to re-seed that area of the lawn.

Cracking

This is very common in hot dry weather. You will see long cracks appearing in the lawn surface as the soil dries out. There is nothing you can do about it beyond waiting for the rain to come.

Dead grass in the summer

Hot dry spells during the summer will dry out lawns and turn the surface brown. It looks unsightly but the lawn will quickly recover after there has been some rain.

Moles

A line of small hills of newly turned earth across the lawn indicates the arrival of the dreaded moles in your garden. The only good thing is that the soil they have dug up makes a nice soil conditioner when placed on your flowerbeds. Getting rid of moles is much harder, especially if you are a bit squeamish about catching them. The best option is to use a sonic mole detector which emits a high pitched noise underground and drives them away, or to plant some mole bulbs encouraging the mole to leave your garden. Moles do not like the smell of the bulbs and even when the bulbs grow and flower they are low growing and blend in with the lawn so do not look out of place.

Moss

Moss will often grow in shady or damp areas of the lawn. Apart from making the lawn look unsightly it can make the surface slippery so you do need to remove it. Use a lawn rake to scrape it away and allow the moss to dry out before adding to compost bins or putting in hanging baskets and pots to help retain moisture in the soil.

Snow and frost damage

Yellow and patchy lawns can result from heavy snowfalls and bitter winter temperatures and show that damage has occurred. If this has happened, you need to feed the lawn and add some new lawn seed into the existing grass. Use a lawn rake to scrape away the dead grass and loosen the surface of the soil before spreading a mixture of lawn seed and fertiliser.

Lawn watering

With all the talk of global warming and water shortages, watering the lawn has become a very controversial issue. It takes a lot of water to keep grass alive during the summer and it is usually one of the first things to be forbidden by water authorities. Watering a lawn is not an essential task as even if a lawn looks dry and brown, it will recover quickly after a shower of rain and new shoots will quickly appear.

There are simple measures you can take to maintain the appearance of a green lawn for as long as possible during the summer. The key is taking action early enough. So what can you do?

- Avoid watering your lawn completely. If you do not water the lawn, the grass will automatically form longer deeper roots as it seeks out any source of moisture in the ground and becomes naturally more drought resistant.

- Use a higher cut when mowing to leave grass stems at least 7.5cm high.

- Consider using a mulching mower which will chop up grass stems into tiny pieces before returning them to the soil to provide a natural mulch and food for the lawn.

- Identify any areas of compacted soil within the lawn in spring and aerate them by using a garden fork to pierce holes in the soil before brushing in a little sand. This will help strengthen the grass roots by giving them better access to food and water.

'Watering a lawn is not an essential task as even if a lawn looks dry and brown, it will recover quickly after a shower of rain and new shoots will quickly appear.'

Summing Up

- Use the basic lawn care steps to keep your lawn looking healthy.

- Keep some grass seed handy to fill in any bare patches.

- Avoid watering your lawn completely so the grass naturally forms deeper roots and becomes more drought resistant as a result.

Chapter Seven

Bargain Hunting

At first glance, gardening, especially if you are creating a new garden, can seem very expensive. If you are not careful, hard landscaping can easily take up most of your budget and a visit to the local garden centre can arouse dismay at the cost of buying shrubs, trees and other plants. Fortunately, there are ways to keep costs down. You don't have to spend lots of money to have a nice garden.

Only buy the really essential tools and equipment that you need for the garden. There are lots of gardening gizmos and gadgets on sale in garden centres or the Internet but most of them are not really necessary when caring for a garden. Shop around for bargains and visit some car boot sales – it is surprising what you can find. I have seen everything from tools, stakes, fencing wire and plants on sale. However, take care when buying second-hand tools, make sure they're safe to use and actually work.

Hard landscaping is the most expensive part of any garden. If you are doing it yourself, visit a range of DIY stores, garden centres and builders' merchants to see what is available and get the best value. Generally, expect the most decorative finishes to be the most expensive.

It is worth looking on the Internet as you may be able to get gardening items free of charge as long as you can collect them. Freecycle is a wonderful not-for-profit-organisation that aims to match people who have things they want to get rid of with people who can use them, in order to reduce the amount of material going into landfill sites (see help list).

V skips is another useful recycling organisation. Instead of throwing items away in a skip, you can create a virtual skip where others can see what is inside and offer to take them away (see help list).

Checklist

- Make a list of the really essential tools and equipment you are looking for and stick to it, otherwise you can be tempted by things you don't really need.

- Take care buying second-hand power tools – always make sure they are safe to use and do actually work.

- Look for the best-value options by visiting your local shops and using the Internet.

'Begin your search for cheap plants in garden centres by concentrating on their bargain areas where prices are substantially reduced. With a bit of tender loving care, most plants purchased in these sections will thrive in your garden.'

Searching for cheap plants

Begin your search for cheap plants in garden centres by concentrating on their bargain areas where prices are substantially reduced. With a bit of tender loving care, most plants purchased in these sections will thrive in your garden. Garden centres often consign plants to the bargain area because they look a bit untidy, are overgrown or simply outside their main flowering period.

Avoid plants which are severely pot bound. You can identify these plants easily by looking at the roots. Pot bound plants often have lots of roots growing outside the pot, or tightly encircling the inside of the pot. The problem here is that even if you cut off the surplus roots and try loosening the left over roots, they often continue to grow in a circle and do not establish very well in the garden. The other main type of plant to avoid is anything that looks diseased such as roses with lots of rust or black spot on their leaves.

So what should you look for in a bargain area? Search out plants which are a bit overgrown and just need a bit of tidying up and weeding to make them look presentable. Trays of pansies or primulas are often put in the bargain centre after the main spring flowering period. Such trays are a good buy since they will settle quickly into the garden. Cut off any dead pansy flowers and long strands to create a compact plant and they will soon start flowering again, while primulas will flower happily again in the autumn and will continue doing so for many years to come.

Another good buy is to look for pots of overgrown perennials such as asters, hardy geraniums, musk mallow or cornflowers. These can be planted just as they are but it is even more cost saving to split them up to make more than one plant. This is not hard to do. Gently remove the plant from the pot and place it on the ground. You may be able to see immediately where there are clumps of plant with large sections of root that can be pulled away easily from the main plant. If this is not possible, put two garden forks back to back through the centre of the plant and gently pull apart to create two plants. Add plenty of fertiliser and water to the planting hole, and the split plants will become sizeable clumps within a year or so.

Overgrown pots of perennials can often be found throughout a garden centre's plant shelves during the autumn. They may still be on sale at normal prices but they are worth buying simply because you can divide them up at home and get at least two for the price of one.

Plantsreunited.com is an online gardeners' swap shop where people can advertise plants, seeds and bulbs they want to swap or sell. It aims to be a cheap way of locating plants for the garden and is worth investigating to see if there are any plants available near you.

Ask relatives or friends for chunks of perennial plants in the autumn, or for cuttings from plants in their garden. Cuttings will need to be grown on for a few months in pots in a greenhouse or cold frame before being placed in the garden. Dip the cutting in hormone rooting powder and put in a pot of compost, then cover the pot with a polythene bag and tie it lightly at the top. Keep an eye on the cutting and when you see new leaves begin to appear, it is time for you to put the young plant into a bigger pot and place it uncovered in the greenhouse. Let it stay in the greenhouse until the risk of frosts has ended, then let the plant harden off before planting it out.

Another good source of cheap plants is the numerous plant sales held all over the country. These mainly take place in the spring, early summer and early autumn and details can be found in local newspapers or on local notice boards. Such plant sales are often held by local horticultural societies, charities or churches keen to raise funds and some really superb bargains can be

'Plantsreunited. com is an online gardeners' swap shop where people can advertise plants, seeds and bulbs they want to swap or sell.'

found, especially if you are looking for large clumps of plants, small trees or bulbs. In some areas, plant sales are organised by the local branch of the National Council for the Conservation of Plants and Gardens (NCCPG) (see help list). Although NCCPG plant sales usually include stalls from specialist nurseries selling plants at full price, the real bargains are to be found on the stalls where plants have been grown by members and donated in order to raise funds.

Why not enjoy an afternoon stroll around someone else's garden, picking up a few ideas on planting and get a few cheap plants while you are there? Every year, over 3,000 private gardens nationwide are open to the public via the National Garden Scheme, Red Cross and St John Ambulance Open Gardens. Most of these gardens include plant stalls selling very good quality plants grown in the garden or donated by other gardeners and are sold at very low prices. Finding details of private gardens open to the public is quite easy – just look in your local papers, in tourist information centres or get a copy of *The Yellow Book* (The National Gardens Scheme, 2010) from bookshops, the Internet and newsagents. A separate Scottish version is also available.

'Big drifts of bluebells, snowdrops, daffodils and other bulbs look gorgeous under trees or in lawns and can be established cheaply and quickly by buying bulbs by mail order in the late winter/early spring.'

Big drifts of bluebells, snowdrops, daffodils and other bulbs look gorgeous under trees or in lawns and can be established cheaply and quickly by buying bulbs by mail order in the late winter/early spring. At this time there are always lots of advertisements for bulbs 'in the green' – these are bulbs which have already flowered and have begun to die back. Planting bulbs at this stage in their lifecycle will help them to establish quickly and easily – and you can get more for your money than buying small numbers of dormant bulbs in the garden centre every autumn. However, when buying bulbs in the green always take care to only respond to advertisements placed by certified growers – unfortunately many advertisements for bulbs in the green are placed by unscrupulous people who have dug up bulbs from the wild and are damaging the environment for everyone else.

Why not grow your own plants? This is a cost saving method and it does not require a lot of skill. If you feel hesitant about trying to grow your own look for seed packets marked easy to grow or packets designed for children. These packets will have very clear instructions and the majority of seedlings will grow into good sized plants. A bit of patience is needed – the plants do not grow overnight. Use annuals to get quick ground cover during the spring and summer and for filling in gaps between existing plants. The majority of annuals can be grown straight into the soil with very little preparation needed but do make sure that the area is weed free first!

Checklist

- Search out bargain areas in garden centres near you or buy from charity and plant stalls.

- For extra value, divide pots of overgrown perennials to get more for your money.

- Grow your own plants from seed – choose the packets marked easy if you're a bit unsure.

Water recycling

All plants need water to survive and with drier summers becoming the norm, using mains water is becoming increasingly expensive. The answer is to recycle water from elsewhere, especially rainwater. Every gardener should have at least one water butt attached to down pipes taking water from the gutters. Even sheds and greenhouses can provide enough rainwater to fill at least one water butt. Always make sure that lids are kept tight and fit well.

If you are creating a new garden and having to put in a new path or driveway, it is worth considering bricks laid onto permeable membranes linked to an underground tank. When it rains, water drains through the gaps in the bricks, through the membrane and is captured in a tank providing a reservoir of water that can be pumped out for use in the summertime.

But it is not just rainwater that can be recycled. Water that has been used for cooking, washing vegetables, washing hands, having a bath or doing the washing is known as grey water and this can be used on the garden as long as you take a little care with it. Although grey water will contain small amounts of soaps, detergents and other chemicals these are sufficiently diluted by use that they do not cause any problems as long as you have been using soaps and detergents that are as mild and biodegradable as possible. However, bear

'Every gardener should have at least one water butt attached to down pipes taking water from the gutters.'

in mind that such water may contain pathogens and bacteria. All vegetables crops that have been grown using grey water should be very thoroughly washed before use. If someone in the house has been ill, don't use their bathwater on the garden until they have completely recovered from their illness.

Removing grey water from baths, sinks and showers can be a very messy business if you are scooping it up into buckets and bowls. A useful alternative is to invest in a diverter kit such as the Droughtbuster®, which can be used to channel grey water from the down pipe into the garden, or via suction device attached to a hosepipe through the window. Be prepared for suction devices to take a little time to get the water moving – the effect is not immediate but they do work quite efficiently once the water has begun draining away. For more information, visit www.droughtbuster.co.uk.

Some dos and don'ts to remember when using grey water:

- Do remove all food scraps from washing up water.

'Don't use water unnecessarily, try to conserve as much as possible.'

- Do make sure water used to boil eggs or vegetables has cooled before using on the garden. Hot water will kill the plants, but once it has cooled the nutrients from the boiled vegetables or eggs will be really good for your garden.

- Do check out all your detergents and soaps to make sure you are using only the mildest and most environmentally-friendly brands. Don't use anything that has salt or phosphorus in it – the effect will be to reduce the fertility of your soil rather than help it.

- Don't use kitchen water from washing up after meals as this is usually very dirty and full of grease, oil and chemicals.

- Don't store grey water of any kind as it will get very smelly, very quickly! Use it immediately.

Checklist

- Get a water butt for your garden.
- Don't use water unnecessarily, try to conserve as much as possible.
- Use grey water when you can.

Energy recycling

Most houses need outside lights to highlight driveways and pathways but installing mains electricity fed systems can be expensive. You need to dig channels for the electricity cables and this can mean digging up and replacing part of your path or driveway. Then there is the cost of the electrician – it is illegal for any electrical installations involving mains electricity to be connected by anyone other than a qualified electrician. Fortunately there is another option and one that more and more gardeners are adopting – solar power.

Solar lights are much more reliable nowadays and can incorporate a button so you can opt to store up power for when you really need it. Most solar lights have integral charging panels or batteries and you can even get systems where lights are connected to a standalone panel that can be placed some distance away in an area of greatest sunlight.

Materials recycling

Don't forget to look twice at what you are throwing out in the household rubbish – quite often some of those items can be reused around the garden and save you money.

- Instead of buying seed trays why not punch some drainage holes in the bottom of foil or polystyrene trays from ready meals and fill them with compost and seeds?

- Cardboard tubes from the centre of toilet rolls can be tightly packed together on a plastic tray and used as pots for growing seeds. When the seedlings are ready to be planted out, all you have to do is put the tube and plant straight into the garden as the cardboard will rot down naturally, adding nutrients into the soil.

- Yoghurt pots are often used as containers for seeds and seedlings or you can cut them into strips and use as labels.

- With a bit of imagination you can turn almost anything into a plant container – chimney pots, tyres, dustbins, shoes, Wellington boots, even chairs and old car parts! Just make sure there is enough drainage and room for compost and you can start planting.

'Don't forget to look twice at what you are throwing out in the household rubbish – quite often some of those items can be reused around the garden and save you money.'

- Old CDs can be usefully used around the garden as reflectors along a dark path, or you can turn them into bird scarers by tying them onto stakes and let them move in the wind.

- One of the most effective growing supports for runner beans I have ever had was made up of an old rotary washing line turned upside down.

- Old tights make good plant or tree ties, while orange nets are ideal for storing onions in the wintertime.

Summing Up

- Go bargain hunting for plants and tools to reduce your gardening costs.

- Recycle and reuse – both water and energy can be saved if you are savvy.

- Household rubbish can be turned into all manner of useful garden items if you get creative.

Chapter Eight

Propagation

One of the most inexpensive ways of obtaining new plants is to create your own by dividing plants or taking cuttings. The big advantage to this is that the plants will be exact replicas of the original plant, so you will know exactly what they will be like. You can often deal with two tasks at once as many cuttings can be taken from branches and stems when you carry out the annual pruning of shrubs.

Dividing plants

This is the simplest method of propagating perennial plants. It is ideal for bulking up ground cover plants and creating large swathes of colour, as well as rejuvenating established perennials. Autumn is the best time for dividing plants as they will have made lots of growth throughout the summer and will be on the point of dying down for the winter. Often you can find large pots of perennials on sale at quite low prices in autumn, as the garden centres seek to clear stock which will be harder to sell the following year. Buying these pots and dividing them up can easily create two or three plants for the price of one and by summer next year the plants will be quite sizeable.

So how do you divide a perennial plant? You need two garden forks placed back to back in the centre of the plant. Gently pull the forks apart and they will break the plant into two. Depending on the size of the plant, you may be able to divide it further but make sure that each segment of plant has a good collection of roots with it. Replant immediately, adding some fertiliser to the soil and plenty of water. Leave it to settle down and grow.

'Autumn is the best time for dividing plants as they will have made lots of growth throughout the summer and will be on the point of dying down for the winter.'

If the plant has very fleshy roots you will need to use a slightly different technique – chop it up with the blade of a spade! This sounds harsh but as long as there are plenty of roots on the plant it will survive and re-grow.

Sometimes perennials need rejuvenating. This is very common in existing gardens where the plants have been in place for a while. You will see bare patches appearing in the centre of perennials with lots of new growth all around it. All you have to do is dig up the plant in the late autumn and cut away the bare centre part. Break up the outer sections into a suitable number of pieces. Then add some fertiliser to the soil and replant all the outer sections. These will grow together to make a large clump by the following year.

'Get to know your plant before taking cuttings as the timing is all important. It is also essential to have a clean, sharp pair of secateurs.'

Checklist

- Divide perennial plants in autumn. Replant them immediately, adding fertiliser and water.

- If you're cutting roots use a sharp tool – the edge of a spade is ideal.

- Rejuvenate tired perennials by removing dead patches in the middle of the plant.

Taking cuttings

Get to know your plant before taking cuttings as the timing is all important. It is also essential to have a clean, sharp pair of secateurs.

Hardwood cuttings

These are taken from trees and woody shrubs including fruit bushes, dogwood and forsythia. You take the cutting in the winter when the plant is dormant. Cut a pencil-thick stem, cutting only from the previous summer's growth which can be recognised because it is lighter in colour than the rest of the stem.

- Trim the cutting to create a stem about 20cm long, making sure there is a bud at the top and one at the bottom.

- Push the cutting into the ground leaving about 5cm above the soil level so as to give plenty of buds above and below to create roots and stems.

- Firm down the ground around the cutting and water in.

- Keep an eye on it and leave it alone for a year. After this time, you can dig it up and replant wherever you need it in the garden.

Softwood cuttings

These are taken from shrubs and flowers during May and June when stems are soft and pliable. It is a good way of quickly increasing your stock of bedding plants as well as some vegetables like tomatoes, as softwood cuttings can take very quickly and may flower the same year. There are two ways of propagating softwood cuttings.

You can simply pop a stem into a vase of water and leave for a few weeks. It will develop a collection of white roots and all you have to do is quickly put the cutting into a very wet compost and leave them to grow on. The biggest danger in this method is that the stem may get too wet and begin to rot.

To avoid this you can use a rooting hormone which is available in either a gel or powder format. This is a fungicide which encourages the cutting to develop roots while discouraging rotting.

'Take care to check the cuttings regularly and remove any that show signs of rotting.'

- Dip the end of the cutting in the rooting hormone and push the stem into a pot containing potting compost. Firm the soil around it and give it some water.

- Put the pot into a plastic bag and fasten at the top to retain moisture inside.

- Keep the pot in a warm but not hot place and leave to grow.

Take care to check the cuttings regularly and remove any that show signs of rotting. As soon as you see new growth appearing, remove the plastic bag. If there is more than one cutting in the pot, you will have to separate the cuttings into individual pots or plant out as soon as roots start emerging from the bottom.

Semi-ripe cuttings

The right time for taking a semi-ripe cutting is during July and August when stems have begun to harden. It is easy to tell if a stem is suitable because it will bend, not snap, and should not have any flowers on it.

The most effective way of propagating semi ripe cuttings is to use a rooting hormone as described under softwood cuttings. The major difference is that when the cuttings have rooted you will need to grow them on in pots for much longer. All semi-ripe cuttings will need to spend the winter in a cold frame or greenhouse before you can plant them out the following year.

Root cuttings

Root cuttings are the best way of propagating perennials which have long tap roots such as comfrey or verbascum. To do this, you simply cut off a piece of root and replant it. If you want lots of cuttings from the same plant, it is best to dig it up in late autumn and take several slices from the root. Always give the parent plant plenty of fertiliser and water afterwards to help it recover.

This method can also be used for perennials possessing spreading roots like mint, catmint and phlox. All you need to do is cut sections of root into approximately 10cm lengths and place them lengthwise into pots. Cover with a little compost and shoots will soon start to emerge all along the cutting.

All root cuttings should be kept in a greenhouse or cold frame for at least a year before you plant them into the garden.

Checklist

- Make sure you use sharp secateurs.
- Have patience – cuttings will take time to create new plants.
- Remember, not all cuttings will survive so don't be discouraged if your first attempts fail.

Collecting seed

Plants automatically create lots of seeds as this is their way of continuing their species. Collecting seed for use the following year requires just a little bit of preparation but the important thing is to remember to keep the different types of seed separate. Depending on the plant variety, seeds can be collected from mid summer onwards, although autumn is the usual time. Choose a sunny day and look for dry seed heads on your plants, the seed usually tumbles naturally from the dying flowers out of these seed heads. Pick the seed heads and place immediately in a labelled paper bag and leave to dry.

It will take a few weeks for the seed heads to fully dry out. At that point, you need to separate the seeds from the seed heads, this is easily done but choose a day that is not windy. Gently crumble the seed heads into a bowl, then toss the contents lightly in the air blowing softly as you do so. The seeds will fall back into the bowl and the unwanted, lighter seed heads will be blown away. Store the seeds in labelled packets, and place in an airtight container.

Seeds you have collected yourself should be sown in the winter or spring, depending on the hardiness of the plants, for example, the seed from half-hardy annuals should not be sown until late spring. It is best to use self-collected seed as quickly as possible.

Summing Up

- Taking cuttings and collecting seed is a low cost way of increasing your plant stock.
- Make sure you use sharp tools for the job.
- Take more cuttings than you need – not all will survive.
- Store seeds in airtight containers.

Chapter Nine

Maintenance and Problem Solving

Depending on the size of your garden, maintaining it should take no more than a few hours each week. Create a weekly checklist of things to do so that you do not forget anything, and after a while these tasks will become automatic. The tasks will vary according to the seasons. See below for some examples of what should be on your weekly checklists.

Spring – weekly checklist

- Remove weeds from flower and vegetable beds.
- Begin mowing the lawn on a weekly basis in late spring.
- Check any seedlings in the greenhouse.
- Top up the compost heap.

Summer – weekly checklist

- Mow the lawn.
- Remove weeds from flower and vegetable beds.
- Remove dead flower heads from annual plants to encourage longer flowering.
- Harvest any vegetables, soft fruit and berries that are ready.
- Water the plants on a daily basis if required.
- Top up the compost heap.

Autumn – weekly checklist

- Remove weeds from flower and vegetable beds.
- Harvest vegetables and tree fruit.
- Top up the compost heap.

Winter – weekly checklist

- Check plants in greenhouses to ensure they have enough water.
- Cover tender plants, such as apricots, with fleece as protection against any frost that is predicted.
- Remove weeds from flower and vegetable beds.
- Top up the compost heap.

It is not just a matter of maintaining the plants within your garden. You also need to keep tools and equipment well maintained. If they become blunt, it will make gardening much easier. This can be done quite easily by filling a container with sand and adding some used cooking oil. Put forks, spades and hoes into the sand and move them around. This will decrease the risk of rust occurring and keeps the tools sharp.

Plant care

- Check plants regularly as this will enable you to see immediately if any problems are emerging.

- Cut back dead stems back to ground level and remove leaves to the compost heap in late winter, leaving the ground ready for new spring growth.

- Annuals and repeat flowering roses should be dead headed on a regular basis in order to encourage more flowers to appear.

- Other plants are best left to seed as the seed heads and berries can be very pretty and lead to naturally grown new plants in future years, or you can collect the seed as described in chapter 8.

- The leaves and dead flowers on bulbs should be left alone at least six weeks after flowering has ended to allow the bulb to recoup nutrition and food from the dying leaves.

'Cut back dead stems back to ground level and remove leaves to the compost heap in late winter, leaving the ground ready for new spring growth.'

Pruning

This has to be one of the biggest worries experienced by any gardener as there is always the fear you could be cutting too much and the plant will never recover. In reality, there is little to fear as to cause irreversible damage, pruning would have to be really drastic. Most plants actually like being pruned.

Although emergency pruning to remove damaged branches can be done at any time, the best time for pruning is in the autumn and winter. This gives the plant time to recover before growth restarts in spring.

The key to successful pruning is never to do more than is absolutely necessary.

- Begin with cutting away any dead wood, followed by branches that may be obscuring paths or growing into other plants.
- Then step back and look at the plant and see what else needs doing.
- Remove any weak branches and any branches that cross other branches.

Trees and large shrubs

Approach these with care and always cut branches in sections from the tip to the trunk. This reduces the chance of branches falling on you, as well as ensuring that all cuts are kept smooth and clean reducing the possibility of damage to the trunk of the tree.

If you have large trees to prune or cut back it is better to call in a specialist who has the right equipment and skills to cut trees safely.

'All new bushes should be pruned when you plant them to give them the greatest chance of establishing themselves quickly.'

Roses and small shrubs

If the bush is very thorny always make sure you wear strong gloves and do not bend too close to the branches. In general, aim to cut back rose branches by a third of the length.

Other shrubs only need light pruning, trimming back only the most recent growth. Lavender, for example, will not re-grow if you cut back to the oldest wood, but enjoys a light prune of the latest year's growth.

Fruit bushes

If you are rejuvenating old bushes, the best way to do this is to cut out all dead wood and reduce the number of stems by a third. All new bushes should be pruned when you plant them to give them the greatest chance of establishing themselves quickly.

Moving trees and shrubs

There are inevitably times when you realise that you have made a mistake when planting a tree or shrub. Do not despair – young trees and shrubs can be dug up and moved to a new, more appropriate spot as long as you do it at the right time and give them enough care and attention.

Trees should only be moved in late autumn or winter. Most shrubs can be moved at any time of the year except during high summer when it is very dry.

Once you have identified the tree or shrub you need to move, preparations need to start the day before you actually move it. Soak the soil thoroughly the day before moving. On the day, dig up the tree keeping as much of the root system intact as possible, especially the thin delicate roots that absorb water. When planting in a new hole put some fresh compost, fertiliser and water in the base of the hole. This will give the plant a good start in its new home.

Carefully replant the tree or shrub at the depth it was previously. If you have moved a tree you will need to stake it for added support. Just before filling in the hole put a stake about one third the height of the tree beside it. Attach a tree tie between the tree and the stake to hold the tree firmly in place. Keep the newly planted shrub or tree well-watered in dry spells for the next year and remove any weeds that grow nearby.

Watering

Plants need water to survive and in dry spells you will need to provide water on a regular basis. As most households now have water meters, using tap water is an expensive option. It is better by far to concentrate on collecting rainwater and reusing grey water from cooking or washing.

When you buy a water butt always make sure that it has a lockable lid so that children and wildlife cannot get in. The presence of a lid will also help keep the water clean and free of slime or leaves. Water butts should be placed under all downpipes leading from gutters on the house, greenhouse and sheds to collect all the water draining from the roofs. Make sure there is an overflow pipe to drain away surplus water or add a connecting water butt.

'When you buy a water butt always make sure that it has a lockable lid so that children and wildlife cannot get in.'

If you are using hose pipes or watering cans, the best time to water plants is in the early evening when the temperature is dropping as this will ensure the majority of the water reaches the plants rather than evaporating into the air and plants have time overnight to drink up the water from the soil. Take great care if you are watering young plants and seeds as they can be damaged or washed away if the flow of water is too strong. The best way to avoid this problem is to use a fine rose on a watering can, arching the water over the plants so that it falls naturally from above. If you need to soak the soil, direct the water only at the base of the plant.

Sprinklers are increasingly frowned upon as they use a tremendous amount of water – around 1,000 litres an hour. Gardeners usually need a permit to be able to use one. Soaker hoses are by far the better answer. These are hoses that have holes at intervals along their length allowing water to trickle out and into the soil. All you have to do is attach it to a water butt or tap and turn the water on very gently so that it just trickles through. Don't forget to cover the hoses with soil or a thick layer of mulch if they are being left in place for regular use as there is no point in allowing water to evaporate.

If you have lots of containers and hanging baskets it is worth considering investing in an automatic drip feed watering system. These comprise a tube and a series of individual nozzles that are directed to send water to containers automatically; you can even find systems which have an inbuilt timer so that it can be switched on to work even when you are on holiday.

Capillary matting is the best way of keeping greenhouse plants well-watered. It is quite simple to use since all you need to do is place the matting on the surface, then put the pots and trays on top of it. Soak the mat really thoroughly once a day and plants will use the water in the mat as a reservoir to take up liquid as they need it during the day.

Checklist

- Water your garden in the evening to reduce the amount of water evaporating.

- Use water butts with lockable lids.

- Do not use sprinklers.

Watering tips

Watering is a time consuming chore so it is important to reduce the amount you have to do as much as possible.

- Don't water your lawn – lawns take up an enormous amount of water to stay green and it is not really necessary to help them survive. Lawns recover naturally from periods of dryness; even if they appear brown and dead, the arrival of rain will quickly ensure that new shoots appear.

- Choose your watering programme carefully – vegetable and fruit plants should have priority as these provide food to eat, followed by any plants you have recently planted. Give plants a thorough soaking every other day rather than just a light watering on a daily basis. If you water too much and too frequently, plants will focus on developing shallow roots close to the surface relying on the water you provide, rather than pushing roots down into the soil.

- Remove weeds as they provide competition for the available water, taking it away from your cherished plants.

- Apply a thick layer of mulch around plants to hold moisture into the soil.

'If you water too much and too frequently, plants will focus on developing shallow roots close to the surface relying on the water you provide, rather than pushing roots down into the soil.'

- Make sure the soil around plants is crumbly and loose rather than hard and compacted as crumbly soil allows the water to drain down to the plant roots.

- Create water reservoirs around very thirsty plants. To do this you need to build up a ring of earth around the plant, about 30cm from the stem. Scoop out some soil from within the ring to create a little well that you can fill with water until it is thoroughly soaked. The water will slowly seep through to the roots of the plant rather than draining away across the surface of the soil.

- Take a plastic bottle and pierce small holes in the bottom third of the bottle. Dig a hole beside the plant and place the bottle within it. Cover up the sides with earth. Fill the bottle with water and fasten the top securely. The water will seep out slowly to the plant's roots; all you need to do is check the bottle from time to time and make sure that it is kept topped up with water.

Container and hanging basket watering

These are possibly the most time consuming and thirstiest areas of the garden. Containers and hanging baskets dry out very quickly in the summer as they are exposed on all sides to the heat of the sun. It is not unusual to find you have to water containers and baskets several times a day and missing a watering session can quickly cause plants to wilt. To make matters worse, as soon as the compost starts to dry out it begins to shrink – and does not expand quickly when you re-water, thus allowing the water to drain away rather than helping the plants. To avoid this problem, you need to take action as quickly as possible.

If a container or hanging basket is suffering from severe dehydration and the compost has begun to shrink, put it immediately into a bucket of water in the shade. Leave it there until the compost has expanded and the plant is no longer wilting.

Water retaining gels can make a tremendous difference to the watering requirements of containers and hanging baskets. These are gels which you mix into the compost, ideally when planting but with care they can be added in at other times. The gels swell up when water is added and then release it slowly as required by the plants.

'Water retaining gels can make a tremendous difference to the watering requirements of containers and hanging baskets.'

Need2Know

Look at where you have placed your containers and baskets. Is there any possibility they can be moved out of the sun for a while during really hot weather? Unless they are drought and sun loving plants, this will immediately reduce some of the stress on the plants making it easier for them to cope with less water. Grouping containers together reduces the amount of heat around plant roots but make sure that small pots are not overshadowed by big ones otherwise they run the chance of not getting enough water when being watered.

Checklist

- Collect as much rainwater as you can for watering during the summer – it's a free resource unlike tap water.

- Soak plants thoroughly every other day rather than giving a light sprinkling each day.

- When planting your hanging baskets, use a water retaining gel to avoid your plants drying out in hot weather.

Pests

No matter how well you care for a garden there will always be problems that arise. Pests are all too common but the key is recognising what the problem is and knowing how to deal with it quickly.

'Pests are all too common but the key is recognising what the problem is and knowing how to deal with it quickly.'

Pest damage

Pest damage can occur underground as well as above ground. Bulbs are frequently dug up by rabbits and squirrels and eaten as tasty snacks, while grubs attack bulbs from inside making them useless. Seeds and young seedlings are often dug up by rats and mice and eaten. It is easy to see when this has happened because the tops of the seedlings are left scattered around the soil or the seed tray, all the mice and rats want are the seeds at the base of the plant. They love sweet corn, pea, sweet pea, pumpkin, courgette and bean seeds. If you think it will be a problem, the best way to prevent it happening is to cover the seed trays or soil area with a layer of garden mesh to make it harder for them to reach the seeds.

Above ground there are lots of potential pests. Rabbits, slugs and snails munch on young seedlings as well as the leaves of older plants. The tips of beans, peas, brassicas and other vegetables are often eaten by pigeons while fruit like strawberries, raspberries and cherries make tasty snacks for birds of all kinds. Rabbits can be a major problem anywhere in the garden, eating plants and digging up bulbs, while in the vegetable patch they will eat anything including onions and have even been known to break down sweet corn plants and eat the cobs!

'Aphid is a general term used to describe greenfly and blackfly, which breed in massive numbers and can rapidly damage plants.'

Aphids are another major pest to gardeners. Aphid is a general term used to describe greenfly and blackfly, which breed in massive numbers and can rapidly damage plants. All aphids during the summer are female and lay large quantities of eggs, which hatch and grow into more egg laying insects within a week. To survive, they suck the sap from plants, weakening plants and making them less resistant to disease and other pests. For example, a rose bush can be attacked by blackfly and within a few days all the leaves have turned black and dropped off, while the rose buds are stunted and may die.

In addition to blackly and greenfly attacks, vegetable areas may be attacked by spider mite, onion fly, carrot fly, cabbage root fly and flea beetle.

- Spidermite mainly attacks tomatoes, strawberries and cucumbers. You can recognise it by the colour of the leaves which turn yellow then brown.

- Onion fly attacks onions and leeks making the plants turn yellow and fall over. This is due to onion fly maggots eating the plant roots and then eating the bulbs.

- Carrot fly shows up as discoloured and wilting foliage. Carrot flies lay their eggs among carrot crops and the newly hatched grubs munch away at the roots.

- Cabbage root fly will attack all types of brassicas including kohl rabbi and cauliflowers. As plants wilt and die, you will see white grubs in the soil around the roots.

- Flea beetle attacks radishes, pak choi, rocket, turnip, cabbages and Brussels sprouts. If you see leaves covered with tiny holes and insects start jumping into the air when the leaves are disturbed, flea beetles are present.

How to deal with pests

Although pests can cause a lot of damage, there are ways in which gardeners can deal with them. Prevention is the best option – taking simple actions at the beginning of any gardening season works better than having to take emergency action. This is the method favoured by organic and green gardeners opposed to the use of chemicals.

Slugs and grubs

Biological pest controls will prevent any build up of slugs and grubs in your soil. These pest controls are tiny worm-like organisms called nematodes which prey on garden pests, like slugs, but cause no damage to wildlife. They are naturally present in the soil but need topping up when there are infestations. Nematodes can be used safely on food crops and in areas where children and pets go.

Using nematodes is simple. You simply mix the contents of the packet with water and cover the affected area. The nematodes work by entering the body of the pest and once inside, they release bacteria stopping the pest from feeding and kill it. The nematodes reproduce inside the dead insect and create a new generation of hungry nematodes that go into the soil to seek more prey. Once they have destroyed the pest infestation, the nematodes automatically die back to their natural numbers.

To get the best results from nematode applications, they should be applied during the evening when the soil does not dry out as quickly, allowing the nematodes time to find their prey. Always make sure that the nematodes are well-watered in by adding extra water after the nematode mixture has been applied.

'Biological pest controls will prevent any build up of slugs and grubs in your soil. These pest controls are tiny worm-like organisms called nematodes which prey on garden pests, like slugs, but cause no damage to wildlife.'

Unused, sealed boxes of nematodes should be stored carefully in the refrigerator until needed. Do not open the pack until you need to use it and always use the entire pack as the nematodes may be unevenly distributed within it.

There are numerous nematode packs which are designed to attack a specific type of insect but the most useful (and simplest) is Nemasys Grow Your Own Fruit and Vegetable Pest Control as it contains a mix of nematodes designed to combat all the major pests such as carrot root fly, cabbage root fly, ants, onion fly, apple codling moth and gooseberry sawfly. One application repeated on a fortnightly basis during the growing season will deal with pests before they reach epidemic proportions.

For small areas such as around vulnerable plants like hostas you can use a slug barrier such as crushed shells, a copper ring or a mulch mat which will deter slugs from entering the area.

Slug pellets are a traditional method of dealing with slugs but there are major risks associated with them as they are chemicals.

- Slug pellets can damage the environment.
- They can harm animals and birds.
- They are not safe around children or pets.
- They can prevent food being harvested.

Slug traps are a safer alternative – the only drawback is that they do need to be emptied each day and refilled with milk or beer. The liquid attracts the slugs who then fall in and drown.

Birds

Birds are lovely and do a great job eating nasty insects but there are times when they will attack crops. Strawberries, raspberries, brassicas and the fresh shoots of peas and beans are particularly attractive to them but fortunately there are various preventative measures you can take.

'Birds are lovely and do a great job eating nasty insects but there are times when they will attack crops.'

The most effective method is to simply put netting over vulnerable plants like peas, raspberries and strawberries. This can be either draped over, or for a more permanent solution, you can install a fruit cage made of metal or wood poles to which netting is fixed. The netting should be removed each winter to avoid snow or wind damage.

Bird scarers can be very effective on a short-term basis. If you have kids it can be fun to make some brightly coloured scarers together, especially ones which will make a noise in the wind. Whatever you use, it is very important to move them around the vegetable plot so that they are not in exactly the same spot more than two or three days at a time otherwise the birds simply get used to them and ignore them!

Mice and rats

If you see rats in the garden and suspect you know where they have made a home, call in the local council pest control people immediately. Rats can be a real nuisance and can give nasty bites. Both mice and rats will dig up and eat seeds that have been planted in the garden or in the greenhouse.

Moles

If you see a line of mole hills heading for your garden, start taking action immediately. The moles will dig up and loosen the roots of anything in their path. Dealing with them is not easy – you can get mole traps but most people dislike emptying them afterwards.

For a gentler method, try scaring them away using electronic mole deterrers which emit a high pitched noise disliked by moles or by planting mole bulbs to make the area unpleasant for them (see chapter 6).

Rabbits

Rabbits are the bane of any gardener and are very hard to deter. The only long-term measure that works is to install a secure fence or netting that they cannot jump over or dig under. In an emergency your best bet is to use temporary barriers such as cloches and cover plants with netting, but make sure they are securely staked down otherwise the rabbits will simply dig underneath. Sonic detectors can be very effective as rabbits dislike the high pitched noise but unfortunately, detectors can be very expensive to use since you need several to protect the crops on all sides and batteries can be used up quite quickly.

Greenfly and blackfly

Ladybirds adore aphids and will happily munch their way through large numbers each day. If you don't have any ladybirds in your garden, you can buy ladybird towers containing larvae that will hatch out ready for feeding. On a long-term basis you can make your garden more attractive to ladybirds and other aphid predators such as hoverflies and lacewings by planting nectar rich flowers like buddleias, marigolds, oregano or the yellow/white poached egg flower. Remove the dead flowers as soon as they have finished flowering and this will encourage more flowers to form.

Onion fly

The best way of deterring onion fly is to grow plants nearby that will affect the insect's sense of smell. Carrots, marigolds and nasturtiums are good choices as they have strong scents which mask the smell of onions. As a further measure, make sure that you do not plant onions in the same place two years running. Rotate the crops around the vegetable patch and this will ensure that the onion fly grubs do not build up numbers in the soil.

Carrot fly

Carrot fly can be a major problem as it can quickly make a crop inedible. Thankfully, there is an easy answer. All you have to do is provide a barrier between the fly and your crops. Carrot fly can't fly very high above the ground so growing the carrots in a raised bed, under fleece or placing some logs, pieces of wood or similar barrier around the carrots will be enough to deter them. Some varieties of carrot do have a greater resistance to the pest, while sowing in early summer rather than spring will mean you miss the peak hatching periods.

'Ladybirds adore aphids and will happily munch their way through large numbers each day. If you don't have any ladybirds in your garden, you can buy ladybird towers containing larvae that will hatch out ready for feeding.'

Cabbage fly

Deter cabbage flies by putting a collar around young plant stems will act as a deterrent to this pest.

Flea beetle

Remove all dead plant debris at the end of the growing season and put it on the compost heap to rot down to stop flea beetles from finding somewhere to hide during the winter. It will reduce the chance of your crops suffering from their attacks the next year.

Checklist

- Identify your garden pest and deal with it quickly.

- Prevention is better than cure.

- Get the timing right when you use biological controls.

Garden ecology

One of the easiest ways of dealing with pests is to encourage nature's own predators to do the job for you. Birds love insects and grubs so adding a few nest boxes and planting some bushy shrubs to provide cover for small birds will quickly encourage them into your garden.

Ladybirds, lacewings and hoverflies need to eat massive quantities of greenfly and other aphids in order to survive. Attracting them is easy if you provide some nectar rich flowers, while a little clump of deadnettle in a corner will be home to an insect that does not attack flowers but makes a wonderful meal for ladybirds. You can also buy ladybird larvae and ladybird towers which will provide homes for them in the winter.

If you have an area that is damp and shady, leave some rotting wood and shady rocks around to encourage toads to take up residence. Slugs are one of their favourite meals, likewise insects and larvae.

'If you have an area that is damp and shady, leave some rotting wood and shady rocks around to encourage toads to take up residence.

Hedgehogs are another wonderful type of predator that need a large supply of insects and beetles throughout the growing season to put on enough fat to survive the winter hibernation. You can encourage them to stay in your garden by making a hedgehog shelter. These are very easy to make from a large wooden or plastic box turned upside down and placed in a shady spot. Cut an entrance hole in one side and place lots of dry leaves inside to form a bed. Cover the box with more leaves and twiggy branches to keep it warm.

Companion planting

This is a very traditional method of deterring pests. Many insects find their chosen plants by following their sense of smell – confuse that sense of smell with the presence of other highly scented plants and the insects go elsewhere. Good combinations in the vegetable patch are onions and carrots and celery, fennel, corn salad and tomatoes.

Other good companion plants which can be used throughout the garden as well as in the vegetable patch are dill, lavender, lemon balm, sage, marjoram, love in a mist, cornflowers, poppies and nasturtiums.

Need2Know

Summing Up

- Prune your plants in autumn and winter to give them chance to recover before growth begins again in spring.

- Cut branches of small trees and large shrubs in small sections for safety reasons.

- Water your plants in early evening and make sure the flow of water isn't too strong. If you water too much too frequently, plants will only develop shallow roots.

- Think about the methods you use to deal with pests in your garden. Where possible try to avoid chemicals.

- Encourage natural predators into your garden so they can get rid of the pests you don't want.

Need2Know

Chapter Ten

Gardening Indoors

Most houses have at least one or more house plants and there is an increasing trend for people to grow salad and baby vegetables on their window sills. There is a wide range of plants available from foliage and flowers to herbs and vegetables that can be grown indoors. Window sills are also a good way of raising plants from seed if you do not have a greenhouse. Keeping indoor plants alive and in good health is another matter!

Choosing plants

Choose your indoor plants with care. Think about where you want to put the plant – is it in shade or a very sunny spot? Do you want a permanent plant that will provide foliage all year round like aspidistra, ferns, dracaena and cordyline? Or do you want plants that flower on an occasional basis in which case African violets, passion flowers, Busy Lizzie and pelargoniums may be a better choice? Or do you want plants and bulbs such as hyacinths and primulas that will flower indoors, but need to be moved into the garden afterwards? All plants need access to natural light but it's important they aren't caught in any draughts, especially if they are flowering. Foliage plants can be more forgiving if they get caught in occasional draughts of cold air.

If you are placing indoor plants on window sills you need to take extra care, especially in winter. When the curtains are drawn at night, leaving plants on the window sill can be a bad idea as it traps the plant beside a cold window. If it gets too cold, it can affect the plant's chance of survival. Be prepared to move window sill plants into the room overnight.

'When the curtains are drawn at night, leaving plants on the window sill can be a bad idea as it traps the plant beside a cold window. If it gets too cold, it can affect the plant's chance of survival.'

Growing seeds on window sills can result in tall, leggy plants bending towards the light and possessing only a few leaves on the lower stems. This is because they are getting an uneven amount of light. To deal with this you need to turn the pots round at regular intervals.

Cacti are a specialised yet very popular type of indoor plant. It is easy to understand why they are popular – you can neglect them yet they will very frequently continue to survive. Although cacti do require far less water than any other indoor plant, to get the best out of them they do require considerable care. For example, Christmas cacti are often given as gifts, but unless you are careful they quickly lose all their flowers and look scruffy, yet with care could flower every year. With the right conditions cacti can flower regularly and look quite spectacular.

'If you are growing plants indoors you will need a supply of pots, compost and trays or saucers on which to place the pots.'

Most cacti prefer to sit outside during the summer rather than being in a stuffy room, and like to be cold in winter. However, Christmas cacti prefer a cool period and less watering after flowering has taken place. During the summer they like to be outside in a shady spot, before coming indoors in autumn and kept dry and cool until the flower buds start to appear. At this point water regularly and keep in a warm – but not hot – room.

Growing indoors

If you are growing plants indoors you will need a supply of pots, compost and trays or saucers on which to place the pots. This is very important because the trays and saucers will allow water to drain from the pots without damaging your furniture. The only essential items that you will need are a watering can, misting spray, stakes and some liquid fertiliser to feed the plant at regular intervals. Plants will quickly exhaust the nutrients contained in the compost and these will need topping up every other week when the plant is growing. A small trowel and fork is useful when it comes to planting but you can just as easily use some old cutlery.

Check your plants every two or three days and remove any dead leaves or flowers. Tall plants may need staking to keep them upright, while climbers can be wound around stakes, trellis or wire hoops. Don't forget to turn the pots

Need2Know

around regularly to ensure that the plants grow evenly and do not lean towards the light. This is particularly important if you are growing plants on the window sill as they can develop weak, leggy stems.

Every few months, check that the plant's roots have not started to grow round in a circular fashion just inside the pot. If this has happened, it means the plant is root bound and needs to be repotted.

- Spread some newspaper onto a flat surface and gently remove the plant from its pot by squeezing the sides and loosening any roots growing out of the bottom.

- Put a layer of compost in the base of a slightly larger pot, then put the old pot inside the new one. Fill up the space between the sides of the two pots with compost and press it down firmly. When you take out the old pot there will be a clear hole in the middle of the compost.

- Gently loosen the roots of your plant and place it in its new home. Give it some water and food, and place in a shady spot to settle down.

All indoor plants will need a rest during winter time. This simply means they need less food and water until the arrival of spring encourages them to begin growing again.

'All indoor plants will need a rest during winter time. This simply means they need less food and water until the arrival of spring encourages them to begin growing again.'

Checklist

- Turn window sill pots regularly to avoid leggy or bent plants.

- Remove any dead leaves and flowers regularly and stake any tall plants to keep them upright.

- Repot your house plants when you notice roots coming through the bottom of the pot.

Watering

Watering is the biggest problem for most people when caring for house plants. It is all too easy to either forget to water plants or to give them too much water. The best advice is to try to get into a routine where you automatically check house plants every other day (or daily during the summer) to make sure they actually have some water. The warmer it is, the quicker the water in pots will evaporate, leaving plants desperate for water. Most plants will need less water in winter than in summer.

When watering, avoid pouring water over the plant itself. Pour the water gently onto the compost. You can gently mist the leaves by using a squeezy spray as this helps keep the leaves free of dust and able to take up energy from the sunshine.

'Keeping a little water in the saucer or container in which the plant is standing will help to maintain humidity as well as providing a source of water from which the plant can drink when necessary.'

If you are uncertain as to whether a plant needs water or not the best way of checking is to use your finger. Touch the surface of the compost and see if it is dry and powdery, then push your fingernail into the compost – if it comes out dry then watering is definitely needed. If the compost has started to shrink away from the sides of the pot, then urgent action is needed and you need to plunge the pot into a container of water big enough to make sure that the water surface is slightly deeper than the pot surface. Leave it in the water until bubbles have stopped appearing, then take it out and let it drain before putting the plant in a cool, shady spot for a day or two.

Keeping a little water in the saucer or container in which the plant is standing will help to maintain humidity as well as providing a source of water from which the plant can drink when necessary.

Pests and diseases

House plants can suffer most of the same pests that prey on outdoor plants such as greenfly and blackfly. The tell-tale signs are holes in the leaves, the presence of aphids on stems, or small black insects flying around a plant and little white maggots seen crawling in the compost. Small webs growing between leaves and stems indicate the presence of red spider mite, especially if the compost is very dry. Misting regularly will help avoid any such problems, but if they occur, the best answer is to use a soap spray from your garden centre.

Most diseases are caused by bad ventilation and poor drainage. Overwatering seedlings and cuttings can make stems turn black causing the stems to fall over and die. Likewise too much water can cause the centre of a plant and the leaves to become soft and rotten.

Above all, remember that frequent misting of the leaves and feeding with a good fertiliser will help keep the plants healthy.

Herbs

Herbs are very easy to grow indoors as well as outside. It is a good way of ensuring you have a good supply of fresh herbs all year round. Mint, for example, will die off during the wintertime so why not dig up a small section of roots and pot them up before bringing them into the warmth. They will quickly send up some new stems and fresh leaves that you can pick as required.

The best herbs for growing indoors are those which can be cut regularly such as mint and basil, low growing herbs like thyme and ones which are very tender, like lemon grass. For beginners, mint, basil and parsley are the easiest herbs to grow. If you have a cat, you could grow catmint – this is a herb which cats love to eat. It is not edible for humans.

Herbs are best grown in separate pots, and placed together on windowsills or in a sunny corner of the kitchen. Evergreen bay trees should be brought inside during the winter, as they are not fully hardy. Remember to turn the pots around on a regular basis so that they do not become straggly, and cut leaves frequently. As long as they are fed and watered regularly; and given new compost at least once a year; indoor herbs can survive for several years.

'For beginners, mint, basil and parsley are the easiest herbs to grow.'

Summing Up

- Turn indoor plants regularly, repot when the roots appear out of the bottom of the pot.

- Avoid pouring water over the plant, instead mist the leaves regularly and gently water directly into the compost.

- Keep plants well ventilated and feed with a liquid fertilizer regularly.

Help List

BBC Gardening

www.bbc.co.uk/gardening
Lots of information can be found on the BBC gardening website.

Drought Buster®

www.droughtbuster.co.uk
Visit the website for information on water-saving devices you could use in your home.

Expert Books

www.expertgardening.co.uk
A series of specialist books about gardening written by a garden expert.

Freecycle

www.freecycle.org
Freecycle is a network to promote waste reduction and help save landscape from being taken over by landfills. It's a great way to find other people's unwanted gardening equipment and plants – you can also add your unwanted items for other people to take if you want to.

Garden Organic

www.gardenorganic.org.uk
The UK's leading organic growing charity. The website is full of advice and information on organic growing.

National Council for the Conservation of Plants and Gardens (NCCPG)

www.nccpg.com
The NCCPG work to protect and preserve plant heritage.

National Gardens Scheme

www.ngs.org.uk
The Open Gardens Scheme raises £2 million for charity every year by opening 3,700 gardens to the public for limited times throughout the year.

Nemasys

www.nemasysinfo.co.uk
You can buy environmentally-friendly nematode treatments to get rid of garden pests from this website. There is also a lot of information if you wish to find out more about the products.

Planning Portal

www.planningportal.gov.uk
Find information on building regulations on this website.

Plants Reunited

www.plantsreunited.com
On this website you can buy, sell or swap your surplus seeds, bulbs, plants, vegetables and equipment, check what others are offering for sale or for swap, and place 'wanted' advertisements for any items you don't seem to be able to find.

Recycle Now

www.recyclenow.com
A great source of information on recycling, including composting.

Red Cross

www.redcross.org.uk
The Red Cross run an open garden scheme across the UK which raises money for their activities all over the world.

St John Ambulance

www.sja.org.uk
St John Ambulance also run an open garden scheme throughout the UK to raise money.

Tree Surgeons Register

www.treesurgeonsregister.com
A directory with a postcode search to find your local tree sureon.

V Skips

www.vskips.co.uk
This is a virtual skip on the Internet, another good way to reuse other people's unwanted items.

Gardeners'

Spring	Summer
Rake the lawn to remove thatch and moss.	Mow the lawn.
Mow the lawn and add fertiliser.	Plant winter flowering bulbs.
Sow your vegetable, annual and perennial seeds.	Plant half-hardy annuals, tender vegetables like courgettes, sweetcorn, French beans, container grown shrubs, roses, climbers and fruit bushes.
Plant summer flowering bulbs.	Water the garden regularly.
Put out cloches or fleece to warm up the soil in the vegetable garden to allow early sowing of seeds.	Ventilate your greenhouse, use white shading on the glass to reduce heat.
Plant perennials, hardy annuals, climbers, shrubs, container grown roses or fruit bushes.	Weed regularly.
Prune roses and climbers.	Cut and dry herbs.
Prune shrubs like Dogwood grown for their winter colour.	Trim and reshape hedges.
Prune spring flowering shrubs immediately after flowering.	
Weed regularly.	
Put mulch around plants.	

Need2Know

Calendar

Autumn	Winter
Plant spring flowering bulbs.	Plant bare root roses, trees and fruit bushes.
Plant bare root roses, trees and fruit bushes.	Prune fruit trees.
Sweep up fallen leaves and place in the compost.	Dig over bare soil and add manure if required.
Move any large plants if you need to.	Remove all debris and dead plants to compost heap.
Protect late crops from light frosts by using cloches or fleece blankets.	Clean the greenhouse.
Clean pools and remove pumps from water features.	Insulate the greenhouse with bubble polythene to save on heating costs.
Stop mowing the lawn.	Clean and repair tools.
Trim hedges.	Take the mower to be serviced.

Gardener's Dictionary

Acid soil
This is soil that has a pH of less than 6.5 and contains very little natural lime. It is not suitable for plants like beech and ash.

Alkaline soil
This soil has a pH of over 7.3 and is sometimes described as chalky or limy. Plants like rhododendrons and camellias (see page 15) will not grow in it.

Annual
These are plants that grow, flower and seed during the summer. They will not survive the winter. Typical annuals include tagates and marigolds (see page 50). They should only be planted in the garden after all danger from frost has passed – usually from June onwards.

Bare root
During the autumn and early winter roses, trees and bushes may be available as bare root plants. These are plants that have been dug up from the fields and must be planted immediately in the garden. The roots are bare and may be wrapped in moss or plastic.

Bedding
Garden centres often refer to trays of low-growing plants (like primulas and pansies) or annual flowers (e.g. marigolds and lobelia) as bedding plants. These are plants that can be used to cover or fill gaps within a flower bed quickly and at fairly low cost. Page 54 covers this in more detail.

Bi-annual
These are plants that can be grown from seed one year, and come into flower, seed and die the following year. Typical bi-annuals are foxgloves, wallflowers and honesty (see page 50).

Bolting
This is a common problem with lettuce and other leafy vegetables that are not harvested frequently. If left, they start growing upwards and develop flower heads, making the vegetables inedible. Bolting can happen at any time but is most common during the summer.

Brassicas
This is a generic name for cabbages and cauliflowers.

Chitting
This is a task undertaken when preparing potatoes for planting. The tubers (seed potatoes) are placed on their sides on a tray or in egg boxes so that the eyes are pointing upwards. Leave the young plants in a light, cool, frost-free place to encourage shoots to appear. Once this happens, the tubers can be planted into the ground.

Cloche
A small portable structure that is used to protect plants against the frost.

Companion planting
Many insects find plants by their sense of smell, so you can confuse them by growing other strongly scented plants nearby. They cannot find the scent they want and so go elsewhere rather than destroying your plants!

Deadheading
Cutting dead flower heads off, this will encourage more flowers to emerge – in other words, you're encouraging the plant to put all its energy into making seeds.

Deciduous
A deciduous tree or shrub will lose its leaves in autumn and new leaves appear every spring.

Earthing up
After potato tubers have been planted in the earth and leaves have begun to appear, use a hoe or spade to pull the earth up to create a mound around each plant. This will encourage the development of a large crop of potatoes. It also keeps the potatoes edible because if they grow too close to the surface they turn green.

Germination
This is what happens when seeds start sprouting and forming young plants.

Hardy plants

These are plants that can be left outdoors all year and will survive frosts. Hardy plants can be perennials, shrubs or trees, examples include irises and hellebores. (see page 49).

Half-hardy plants

These are plants that will survive light air frosts but not heavy ground frosts. You can usually plant half-hardy plants, like sunflowers, outside from April onwards.

Harden off

This is a way of allowing plants that have been growing under cover to get used to outside temperatures by putting the plants outside for increasing amounts of time.

Hoeing

Using a backwards and forwards motion with a hoe, cutting through weed seedlings and preventing them from growing.

Mulch

This is a layer of material, usually bark or compost, which is placed around plants to prevent moisture being lost from the soil. At the same time, the mulch makes it harder for weeds to take root as it cuts out the light needed for them to grow.

Perennial

Perennial plants will re-grow every year from their original root. They usually die down over winter but start growing again in spring. Typical examples are lupins and achillea (see page 49).

pH

This is a unit which is used to measure how much acid or lime is present in the soil.

Plug plants

You can buy plug plants from garden centres in early spring. They are very young plants which have to be grown in greenhouses for some weeks before planting outside.

Pricking out

Seeds which have been grown in pots or trays may need to be moved into new pots when they have developed their first true leaves. This is called pricking out as more growth space is created between the seedlings.

Propagate

When you propagate a plant, you are cloning it by taking cuttings or by collecting seed.

Pruning

When you prune a plant, you are cutting off dead branches and twigs to keep it healthy and to encourage it to grow new strong shoots. Regular pruning can also be used to limit the size of a shrub or tree.

Sub-soil

This is the under-soil that is less fertile and harder to dig.

Thinning

Thinning is a technique used when growing plants from seed. The aim is to create more space for the plants to grow. If young plants are growing too closely together, you remove one or two of the plants. These plants can be replanted elsewhere in the garden or eaten as baby vegetables.

Top soil

This is the very fertile soil in which plants grow.

Transplanting

When you transplant a plant, you are simply digging it up and moving it to another part of the garden.

True leaves

When seedlings emerge, the first leaves are their seed leaves which are very different to their normal ones. The next pair of leaves to appear are the true leaves – the ones that all future leaves will look like.

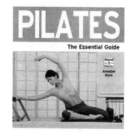

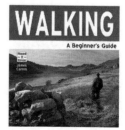

Need - 2 - Know

Available Titles Include ...

Allergies A Parent's Guide
ISBN 978-1-86144-064-8 £8.99

Autism A Parent's Guide
ISBN 978-1-86144-069-3 £8.99

Blood Pressure The Essential Guide
ISBN 978-1-86144-067-9 £8.99

Dyslexia and Other Learning Difficulties
A Parent's Guide ISBN 978-1-86144-042-6 £8.99

Bullying A Parent's Guide
ISBN 978-1-86144-044-0 £8.99

Epilepsy The Essential Guide
ISBN 978-1-86144-063-1 £8.99

Your First Pregnancy The Essential Guide
ISBN 978-1-86144-066-2 £8.99

Gap Years The Essential Guide
ISBN 978-1-86144-079-2 £8.99

Secondary School A Parent's Guide
ISBN 978-1-86144-093-8 £9.99

Primary School A Parent's Guide
ISBN 978-1-86144-088-4 £9.99

Applying to University The Essential Guide
ISBN 978-1-86144-052-5 £8.99

ADHD The Essential Guide
ISBN 978-1-86144-060-0 £8.99

Student Cookbook – Healthy Eating The Essential Guide
ISBN 978-1-86144-069-3 £8.99

Multiple Sclerosis The Essential Guide
ISBN 978-1-86144-086-0 £8.99

Coeliac Disease The Essential Guide
ISBN 978-1-86144-087-7 £9.99

Special Educational Needs A Parent's Guide
ISBN 978-1-86144-116-4 £9.99

The Pill An Essential Guide
ISBN 978-1-86144-058-7 £8.99

University A Survival Guide
ISBN 978-1-86144-072-3 £8.99

View the full range at **www.need2knowbooks.co.uk**.
To order our titles call **01733 898103**, email **sales@ n2kbooks.com** or visit the website. Selected ebooks available online.

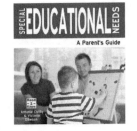

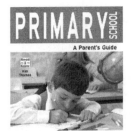

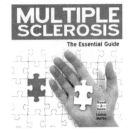

Need - 2 - Know, Remus House, Coltsfoot Drive, Peterborough, PE2 9JX